Whispers

from the

Spirit

Michigan State University
Students Listening to Their
Inner Voice

Dorothy K. Ederer O.P.

NEW PRIORY PRESS

EXPLORING THE DOMINICAN VISION

Dedication

I dedicate this book to my parents:
Ann and Bernard Ederer, my sisters and brothers,
nieces and nephews and grand nieces and nephews.

I dedicate it to the parishioners at
St. John Church and Student Center and to
St. Thomas Aquinas Parish,
and to all students who attend Michigan State University
who are involved in service to others.

Table of Contents

Foreword

At times, all of us have heard a voice deep within urging us to think twice or beckoning us to go forward with confidence. All of us find ourselves in situations filled with uncertainty and doubt. By listening to voices from deep within, we are much more likely to do simply what is "right." We more often than not choose the most humane and generous of acts without regard to what others might think or if anyone else would know.

We are surrounded by noise and pressure. Too often we simply assume that voices can only be heard in solitude or when we pause for reflection. Yet experiences suggest that with total focus, wise choices are sometimes made during the most chaotic moments. Let us not forget that when we make wise choices, it is when we are true and special.

As you read these stories, you will see how often God's Spirit touches the each of our lives uniquely. Many times we experience the different ways that God is urging us into different directions for our lives. God wants us to know how much we are loved and the special plan God has for each of us. Most of the time this can happen when we realize the important part of our praying is really listening.

The following true stories are examples of what can happen to people when they hear that whispering voice within and respond with integrity and authenticity.

Lou Anna K. Simon

Acknowledgement

I could not have had this book published without the help of my Dominican brothers: Fr. Andy McAlpin, whose encouragement and support are always well timed, and Fr. Albert Judy and Terry Rowley who shaped the manuscript into a document ready to print.

A special thanks to Kelly Sandula-Gruner for the exquisite cover design and for Madeline Carino for her graphic designs throughout the book.

Words can't express my gratitude to Polly Lynch and Jean Shane whose expertise in proofreading this manuscript was invaluable.

I also want to thank Lou Anna K. Simon who graciously encouraged and supported the students contributing to this book.
I can't forget the professors and coaches whose encouragement, support and contributions have been valuable.

"'Speak Lord, for your servant is listening.'
We have to be listeners to all her whispers,
because they come in so many different
unexpected persons, places and things.
Be attentive, for it may be she."

Fr. Jake Foglio

Introduction

The following reflections and true stories witness how the Spirit works in our lives. They are living proof of what happens when we open our hearts and listen to the voice within. Each of us hears something different. However, we need to be open and willing to respond.

I chose the title, "Whispers from the Spirit," because of my devotion to the Holy Spirit who is a real and valuable presence in my life. I listened and responded to that inner voice. My mom encouraged us all to let the Spirit guide us in our lives. It is amazing what can happen when you do.

The book is compiled of stories from our students at Michigan State University. As you read their stories you will realize that they are not unique; rather it is often the way God's Spirit touches the lives of each of us. Hopefully, the stories will help you see how the Spirit is working in your life, as you listen with all your heart.

Sr. Dorothy K. Ederer O.P.
Director of Campus Ministry at St. John Student Center

Whisper One: What Is There To Do But Love?

On February 3, 2013, I found myself thinking about a small milestone that would occur the next day. I had been in a relationship for six months. Though not terribly significant, February 4 seemed more important to me because of my previous doubt that I could *ever* be in a relationship for six months, much less reach this point in my senior year of high school. Furthermore, it was certainly not a bad relationship. I had met Shane in band class in my sophomore year of high school (his freshman year). He was kind and caring, a good friend and a hard worker, and cared about his family more than many high school students think possible. Throughout the relationship, he had treated me with the sort of kindness and respect that I did not think I deserved. As with many aspects of life, however, there was one area that made me uncertain about the relationship: though baptized Catholic, Shane had not been raised in or exposed to any sort of faith.

I have always been Catholic, but in high school, I had become a scrupulous, intellectual sort of Catholic, the type who sought out apologetics as if one day hoping to convert the entire world simply through debate. Though I actively sought out resources to learn more about my religion, I found myself unable to pray in any meaningful way. Each night before bed when I tried to pray, I was able to think of nothing other than, "Lord, I'm sorry. I know that I make many mistakes. I don't deserve the blessings you have given me, and am at a loss of words."

By the end of my junior year of high school, I had reached a greater knowledge of the Catholic religion, but a low point in my Catholic faith. I felt unworthy and unlovable. Still, God seeks us most in times like this; and though I could not always feel him near me, I wanted to make sure that I was not going against his will. My relationship with Shane began the summer before my senior year, I sent up a rare, truly genuine prayer: "I know I don't deserve to feel better about life. But if entering into a relationship will make things worse, please stop me. I don't want to be far from you; I just don't know how to come closer."

My relationship with Shane started like any other high school relationship, without any divine intervention to stop us; and by that day in February, I had started to feel better about life and about my boyfriend in many ways, but the barrier between my faith and him had begun to wear me down. And on that day, as I thought about the future and did not see how a relationship could survive without a shared faith, I sent up my second real prayer about the situation: "Lord, I have always felt called to marriage, particularly to motherhood. But sometimes I cannot believe that I will ever be able to answer that call. I just need to know that it's possible—not now, not even years from now, but *someday*—for me to fall in love."

I had no idea how God would answer me, and I felt a little silly. Trying to drop the subject, I went to sleep.

The next day after school, the Monday that marked six months in my young relationship, Shane asked to talk to me on the phone. He sounded nervous, which made me nervous. After a while, he managed to ask the question on his mind: "Could I maybe go to church with your family some time?"

Though faith had certainly been mentioned in our relationship, I had never had the courage to have a real, in-depth discussion with him. That week, as we prepared for our first Mass together, I tried frantically to give Shane an overwhelming amount of information about the Church, realizing just how little I knew myself. We felt nervous and excited as we walked into the church together on Saturday evening. The church building I had attended for my entire life suddenly seemed new as I saw it through Shane's eyes. Each word of the Mass, words that I had been hearing every week for almost eighteen years, seemed new and beautiful and enlightening. After years of trying to be attentive, often unsuccessfully, I was captivated by the Mass; I was falling in love with my faith all over again, or maybe for the first time. I learned later that Shane had been feeling the same way about the Mass; it was the Sign of Peace that really convinced him to keep coming back. He was filled with a sort of peace he had never experienced before, and for the first time, began to believe that it really was the Peace of Christ.

2

The next day, still filled with excitement and fulfillment from the Saturday Mass, I contacted Shane only to receive some bad news. In the early hours of that morning, his grandfather had passed away suddenly and unexpectedly. Naturally, Shane was filled with grief, and I wanted to help him through it. He asked me to come to the funeral on the following Friday for support, and from Sunday to Friday, I tried to support him as much as I could while still balancing a difficult week of school. I shared his grief in a way that I had never thought possible and began to learn what it means to truly care for someone else's well-being more than I cared about my own. By the end of the week, I found myself in tears at night, feeling the weight of his sorrow and my stress and asking God, "How do you expect me to do this? I have never been good at comforting others, and now I am trying to support someone else when I can barely carry my own cross at times...how do you expect me to do this?"

Shane's grandfather was Catholic and involved in the Church; so the second Mass I attended with Shane was a funeral. As I sat in the church with him and his grieving family, feeling out of place and asking God how I could possibly help, we began to sing the Communion hymn, "Make Me a Channel of Your Peace," and one part in particular stood out to me:

> "O Master, grant that I may never seek so much to be consoled as to console, to be understood as to understand, to be loved as to love with all my soul."

To this day, the words of that hymn—the Prayer of St. Francis— remind me of the remarkable change of heart that took place that February, the time in my life when I began to learn how to love God and others. Suddenly, I realized that it wasn't about me. Sometimes God uses us as a conduit of his grace.

Suddenly, I wanted nothing more for my relationship than to bring Shane closer to God; eventually, he ended up doing the same for me. His remarkable leap of faith, his change of heart that came about solely by the grace of God, put my rational, argumentative approach to Catholicism to shame. After the grief of his loss, he began to attend Mass every week, and began to talk of coming into full communion through Right of Christian Initiation for Adults [RCIA]. When we discussed the gravity of the decision, he argued that even though he was young and had little previous knowledge about faith, God had always been present in his life; it was time for him to answer the call and make the relationship two-way.

I went on a retreat in the beginning of April 2014, the month in which Shane completed RCIA and received his First Communion and Confirmation, and I was blessed to be his sponsor. My faith deepened and my life had improved more than I ever thought possible. In a moment of prayer, a question came into my mind, followed by an answer: "Lord, what do you want me to do?" "Do? What is there to do, but love?"

I still want to convert the entire world, but I have come around to a new approach. It is impossible to change hearts simply by changing minds, and it is often impossible to change minds when hearts remain unchanged. All that we can do is love and pray; by the grace of God and the power of the Holy Spirit, we have more than we need to succeed.

The Spirit Whispered: What is there to do but love?

Prayer: Divine Spirit, give me the courage to do your will rather than my own; the courage to accept that I can accomplish anything with prayer; and the courage to approach only you, the source of all love, to find fulfillment, and to pass on that love to others.

Claire Morrison, *Physical Science and Secondary Education*
Grosse Pointe Woods, MI

Whisper Two: "Dominic, Let It Go."

My parents, Rob and Trish Milano, raised my brother, Vincent, and me to be devout Catholics who put our faith with God, at the helm of our lives. I attended religious instruction classes every Sunday before the 11:00 Mass. The problem was that I didn't understand what was being taught to me and frankly, wasn't all that interested. I was that bundle-of-joy who always said the one thing every Catholic parent wants to hear on a Sunday morning, "Do we have to go to Church?" Even though I threw a temper-tantrum, we attended Mass religiously every Sunday despite not getting anything out of it. I give my parents a lot of credit for not giving in to my outbursts.

I was an altar server at Mass for a little over five years because my parents thought it would be very good for me and I was interested in doing it. I remember getting very nervous carrying the cross up to the altar and freaking out that I might drop it or light something on fire while holding the candles like what you would see on America's Funniest Home Videos. Whenever I faced the congregation, a large smile of embarrassment was present on my face. I remember serving at the Christmas Mass when my family came in from Chicago. I was walking towards the altar, my grandmother gave a *very subtle* "AHEM" to get my attention to let me know she was there, causing me to smile and turn red in front of all present. Still, as an altar server, I didn't feel like I got anything out of the Mass and was lost and confused with what our priest was saying.

Fast forward to high school: I still didn't want to go to Mass on Sundays because it was boring. I never told this to my parents because I knew it was one of many fights I would never win. I stopped serving at the Masses my junior year due to the challenging courses I was taking. Even though I never really wanted to go to Mass and was relieved to stop serving, it always felt like something was missing in my life.

A couple years later, I arrived at the greatest school on earth, Michigan State University. I couldn't believe that I was actually in college! I remember it like it was yesterday. My parents helped me set up my room, and went with me on a tour around campus. I met some of my best friends that day: my roommate Corey as I was setting up my stuff in our room; Charles and Kendra in the Holmes cafeteria; Max on the tour of campus; and Michaela and Delania when I helped them set up their router ignoring the fact that I was wearing my Star Wars R2-D2 boxers. I instantly bonded with this group of great misfits. This was one of the first gifts God gave me while starting this new chapter in my life.

It was hard for me when my parents headed home and I knew I wasn't going with them. I shooed them away to spare myself an emotional outbreak. I was homesick within the first week, but when I went to bed that first night, I felt God's presence and he was speaking to me, telling me, "Dominic, everything is going to be okay."

I felt the need to go to Mass, so the first Sunday by myself, I woke up at nine o'clock and walked over to St. John Student Center. I felt so much better after going to Mass. I remember the smiling faces of people welcoming me to St. John's like Sister Dorothy. Bring together the great friends I had made and a great faith community and you've got yourself a nice recipe for a sense of belonging. I felt I was home.

In tough times during school when I did poorly on an exam, I always thought, "That's it, I'm not going to have good enough grades to get into dental school and I'll be a failure in life." My mom always told me, "God works in mysterious ways." I never believed her until I received a 66% on my first college exam. I was listening to Pandora to help calm my nerves and the song, "Let It Go" by Idina Menzel, came on and it just really hit me. I felt in my heart that this was God's way of saying, "Dominic, it is okay. Let this one go. You'll get it next time." And sure enough, I was able to get a 98% on the next exam and aced the class.

During the summer after my freshman year, I attended Mass on Sundays and got so much more out of it than I ever did when I was younger. At the beginning of my sophomore year, I seemed to slowly edge towards my old ways and my relationship with God seemed to slowly dissipate. During this time, I was very interested in writing a book. I searched and searched for ideas of what I could write about and I decided that I could write about all the crazy incidents I encountered as a Resident Assistant (RA) in Holmes. Unfortunately, this was going to be a long process and I wanted to find a way to get something published. My mom's words from my childhood were again illustrated when God presented me an opportunity through Sister Dorothy, to contribute a story for the "Whispers From The Spirit" book. She told me about the book and suggested that I write a story about a time when God spoke to me. The story you are reading is that story.

God is always listening to our secret desires, even though we may think differently. God works in mysterious ways, but in the end, the hardships we endure and the pain we feel will be worthwhile.

The Spirit Whispered: I know you have encountered hardships. However, I want you to continue to trust in me. I have plans for you that are beyond your wildest dreams. Put your faith in me and everything will be just fine. I am always here for you!

Prayer: Divine Spirit, bless those who seek your wisdom and your guidance. Please show us the path to happiness through our faith in you.

Dominic Luke Milano, *Chemistry*
Bridgman, MI

"The Spirit Whispers is the voice
within each of us.
Silence and solitude amplify the
Spirit Whispers.
Be quiet and listen to the Spirit Whispers."

Dr. Ron Cichy, O.M., Professor
School of Hospitality Business at MSU

Whisper Three: Trust in God, You'll Find Hope

Not once does the Bible say, "Worry about it," "Stress over it," or "Figure it out." But over and over it clearly says, "Trust God." The hardest and scariest events in your life are when you need to trust in God the most.

My dad is the hardest working man I know. He has worked his tail off to support and provide for our family of six. He is professional, dependable, and truly a role model for our family. When I was a sophomore in college, he accepted a new job as a salesman for a construction company. He immediately excelled with his enthusiasm and desire to serve his customers. Within six months, he was promoted to branch manager, something almost unheard of for this particular company. He gained more power, a heavier work load, more responsibility, and a large team reported to him. He worked 12-hour days, five days a week. Yes, his paycheck was fatter, but he was sacrificing my brother's football games, my sister's lacrosse games, and other family celebrations. But this extra work load was only temporary. He was still considered "new" to the company only being there six months; he was still learning his old job along with this new promotion. Once he got the hang of things, he wouldn't have to work as much. He'd be able to coach my brother's football team, come home for dinner, and have energy to do things on the weekends.

After a year with this company, my dad was fired. No explanation. No review. No income for our family. First came the *shock*, then came the *anger*, and last *hopelessness*. Yes, he had an incredible amount of experience, but he was missing that one thing companies are looking for—missing that piece of paper, his college degree.

I was terrified. I was scared that my siblings would be pulled from their school. I was scared that my mom would have to stop taking classes. Scared the family might have to move if he couldn't find anything local. Being away in college only made my anxiety worse. In class, all I could think about was my family, especially my dad.

I was working as the Retreat Intern for St. John Catholic Church and Student Center in East Lansing, Michigan at that time. A week after my dad was fired, the planning for our annual Fall Retreat began. It was appropriately themed: *Trust in God, You'll Find Hope.* Every week, I would hear from the other leaders about their experiences and how they *trusted* in God. How they surrendered themselves and put their problems in God's hands. How they overcame their fears and found hope. Praying at Mass became almost like a meditation for me. I would pray to God, "Okay. I'm letting go. I am putting my trust in you Lord. Please help my family. We need you. I trust you." I would say this over and over until I believed it. I pictured it like a trust fall. I needed to completely let go of everything, and fall into God, and trust that He would catch me.

About a month after he was fired, my dad found a new job. My prayers were answered! I felt like God embraced me with open arms. He embraced my whole family and blessed us.

So, what do you fear? What are you scared of? It's okay. No one knows what is going to happen. What we do know is that it's all part of God's plan. Things won't happen overnight, but God will help. Are you ready to trust fall into God?

The Spirit Whispered: I've got this.

Prayer: Divine Spirit, help me to trust you in my darkest hour. When everything seems hopeless, shine your light. Help me remember to offer my troubles to you. Lead me in the right direction. With your help Lord, I can do anything.

Addisen Carino, *Marketing*
Fenton, MI

Whisper Four: You Are Not Alone

Everyone has times in their lives when they feel alone, like no one around them really cares about what they say or what they do or if they are even there at all. It can be really difficult to keep a positive attitude about anything when it seems like you have no one to go to. For me, this period of aloneness came during my first few weeks at Michigan State University.

Before coming to Michigan State University [MSU], I attended a small Catholic high school where my dad was a teacher and I knew the first and last name of every student in the school. Part of the appeal of Michigan State, when I was choosing which college to attend, was that it was so big, full of new people and opportunities. MSU is filled to the brim with people, some wonderful and some not-so-wonderful, but they didn't all come up to me as soon as I arrived and tell me right then and there we were going to be friends.

In the first few days I was at school, I did meet plenty of people, like my roommate, who spent almost all of her time with her boyfriend from high school, and the girl next door to us who complained that she didn't want classes to start because then she couldn't get high all the time. Most of the other people I met were just blurs, names, and faces I wouldn't remember, and they wouldn't remember me either. I so badly wanted to make a good impression on people so they would like me and we would become friends. Friendships don't just happen instantly though, and I wasn't about to share my actual thoughts and feelings with people I just met, especially when it felt like all the other people were so well adjusted, already having the time of their lives in college.

Thankfully, I did have some wonderful supports, my family, and my faith. I called my mom and dad, often multiple times a day. While they both reassured me that I would eventually be fine and make friends and stop getting lost on my way to class, the fact that they were six hours away from me was difficult. A phone conversation can't quite replace a hug. I also did a lot of praying during my first

11

weeks at MSU. At first my prayers were hopeful, but that slowly changed.

"Dear God, thank you for the wonderful opportunities I'm sure I'll find at MSU."
"Dear God, bless the people in my classes and maybe help some of them to actually talk to me."
"Dear God, please help me to be strong and not cry in front of my roommate and her boyfriend again tonight."

After two weeks of what I had hoped would be the best experience of my life, I felt alone and defeated. My family had come to visit me, but they couldn't stay with me forever. I failed my first Chemistry quiz, and still couldn't find my way around. To make matters worse, I got sick, so breathing through my nose was difficult, and my voice was hoarse. I didn't have anyone at MSU I felt like I could really talk to, especially in my terrible hoarse voice. I prayed the best sort of prayer that I could manage at that moment, "Dear God, I know you're with me and listening to what I say, but I don't feel it. I just feel sick and overwhelmed and so alone."

While I had been crying on the phone with my mom earlier that day about being sick, she convinced me that I should go to the doctor. Things would look brighter when I was feeling better. I didn't really believe her, but I went ahead and scheduled an appointment, looked up the best way to get there, then set out.

During the walk from my dorm to the health clinic, I saw so many other people walking, going about their daily lives, not caring at all that I was sick and miserable. All I wanted was to go home and get a big hug from my mom and not have to feel alone anymore. I walked into the clinic and went up to the smiling receptionist. "How can I help you?" she asked me. I tried to explain about my sore throat and congested sinuses, but all that came out was a flood of tears. Quickly, the receptionist got up from behind the desk and gave me a big hug. It was the first hug I received since my mom and dad left on Sunday, and it was so comforting. I cried on her shoulder for a while, and just feeling someone else's arms around me made it that much better. Once my sobs faded to sniffles, the receptionist asked me if I had an appointment and I nodded. She took my name, then gave me hers. "I'm Rebecca," she said. "And I spent most of my first two weeks of college crying, too."

My appointment was relatively short and straightforward. Rebecca showed me to an examination room, and gave me another quick hug, then the doctor game in. She looked in my ears and throat before telling me I had a sinus infection. She gave me a piece of paper with the over-the-counter medicine she recommended. I mumbled thanks and left the examination room, determined to get the medicine, then lay in my bed and cry a while longer where no one else could see me.

I was almost to the door of the clinic when I realized the flaw in my plan. I had no clue where the nearest pharmacy was. Trying not to let this small bump bring out the tears again, I slowly turned and walked back to the friendly receptionist. "Could you please tell me where I could buy..." I squinted at the doctor's stereotypically messy handwriting "a nasal decongestant like Sudafed?"

Rebecca started explaining how to get to Walgreens, but then noticing my hopeless face at the thought of having to find someplace else I had never been. She said, "If you don't mind waiting ten minutes for my shift to end, I could drive you there, and then we could go get ice cream."

God is always with us, even though he isn't physically present. Sometimes, it's enough to know that he is with us in Spirit. But sometimes, particularly when we are feeling sad, sick or alone, he makes his presence known to us through other people. The Spirit whispered to me that day through Rebecca, through her funny story about her mom's homemade remedies for sinus infections; through driving around and showing me some of the important places to know around campus; through her simple acts of paying for my $2.50 ice cream cone; and giving me a hug. The fact that Rebecca was willing to take time out of her busy day to spend time with me, to listen to my problems, and share that her own college experience which wasn't perfect either. God made his presence known to me for the first time in East Lansing, Michigan.

13

As the year progressed, I met other people who cared about the things I said and did, who supported me through challenges, laughed at my jokes, and shared my college experiences. I made friends who helped me feel at home at MSU, the wonderful type of friends who God works through every day. But on that day in early September 2013, when I needed it most, God worked through a woman I didn't know and haven't seen since. That was when the Spirit whispered, "You are not alone."

The Spirit Whispered: I am always with you. I come to you in many different forms, but I am always there, helping you to face the difficulties you may encounter.

Prayer: Divine Spirit, you are always with us, loving and supporting us in all we do. Help us to see you in everyone we encounter, and to be your presence to those who need it most.

Laura Hesse, *Chemistry*
Madison, IN

Whisper Five: The Bumble Bee

Everyone says that your junior year of high school is the hardest. You have to take the ACT test and start applying to colleges. My junior year was definitely the hardest year of my life so far, but not just academically. I have always been a very family-oriented person. I had never lost anyone close to me. This would be the year that I would feel true loss.

My Grandma "B" was a talented and loving person. Every time I called her, she answered with, "Well hello there, dear!" We called her Grandma "B" because her last name started with the letter "B." But soon, the "B" became a symbol of its own. Bumble bees were her signature. If you looked closely, you would notice little things with bumble bees on them around her house. Whenever anyone asked her about her bumble bee key chain, she would explain it was because her three grandchildren called her Grandma "B." In a way, the bumble bees became a symbol of her love for us.

My Grandma "B" had just turned 71 when she found out she had stage four lung cancer. It all happened so fast. One day she went to the hospital and we thought she only had pneumonia. Within a couple weeks, we found out that her cancer was too far along to be cured and it could not even be treated due to other health issues.

She was in the hospital for two months, then moved into hospice. This put stress on my family, especially my mom, because it was hard for her to see her mother in this deep pain. The stress was hard for me to deal with. I started missing a lot of school because the stress would affect my stomach.

There comes a point in time in these types of situations where there is nothing you can physically do. So I prayed. I prayed alone. I prayed with my mom. I prayed silently in classes during school.

When I came home from school one day and received the news of her passing, I couldn't help but wonder why all of this had to happen. People said it was her time, but why did God decide to make her time so soon? Why did it feel like my heart was breaking? Why was it that only two months ago everything was okay and now it felt like it will never be okay again?

Many tears were shed the day of her funeral, but God graced us with beautiful weather. It was a warm and sunny spring day. After the funeral, my brother and I took my eight-year-old cousin outside. The boys were swinging on the swing set in our backyard. I was standing on the patio when the most amazing thing happened.

Something buzzed by me. My first reaction was to feel fear. Then I realized it was a bumble bee. The bumble bee flew around me in a circle. When I was no longer afraid, but in awe, it flew over to my brother and circled around him, then flew to my cousin and circled him as well.

I felt this overwhelming feeling of relief and joy. It was like a message from my Grandma "B" herself. I knew then that everything was going to be okay. I still had a long process of grieving ahead of me, but everything would be okay in time. I knew my Grandma "B" was in heaven and she would be watching over me.

From that day forward, something changed. While wasps and other bugs still induced fear, bumble bees no longer scared me. Seeing one now brings a smile to my face as I remember the day that my Grandma "B" sent one to tell me that she was still there for me.

The Spirit Whispered: Everything is okay. Grandma "B" is no longer suffering. She loves you.

Prayer: Divine Spirit, thank you for being there for us when we are at our weakest. Thank you for showing us that everything will be okay and for helping us make it through our hardest days.

Maddalena Paglia, *Zoology*
Shelby Twp, MI

Whisper Six: You Will Have Peace

I am stubborn, and self-reliant. I was raised Catholic and received the sacraments of Baptism, Reconciliation, Eucharist, and then the year I was to be confirmed, my father wiped out our family financially. It is surprising how quickly a family of four can become a family of three, how someone who loves you can leave you. With no explanation, and with little hope, my mom gathered us in her arms and kept our family afloat. She worked tirelessly, optimistically, and by herself. My mom was our superhero, and it was her and us against the world. When my parents separated, we no longer went to church. My father was a Catholic, his family was the only reason we went to church, and they had hurt us deeply. I blocked out painful memories. I did not pray for help, I did not turn to God. I buried myself in my schoolwork to find success, and hopefully, a college scholarship.

When my mom had saved enough to move us into our own small apartment, I was eager to make friends at my new school. I was craving a sense of normalcy, and needed friends. When Sarah invited me to her house one Friday night, the simple invitation had me smiling all week. I came over around six on a Friday. Sarah opened the door, hugged me, and rolled her eyes saying "It's Friday, so we're going to 'do Shabbat'- but then we can go upstairs." I had never had a Jewish friend, nor had I "done Shabbat." I hoped I wouldn't embarrass myself as the family gathered to pray together to begin the Sabbath. Sarah's mom lit the candles, and Sarah sang a beautiful Hebrew prayer.

Sarah's mom, Gail, placed her hands on the heads of her own two daughters. "Tim, you bless Liz," she whispered. Timothy lovingly placed his hand on my head, as if I was his own daughter, and they began to pray the blessing of the children. They spoke in Hebrew, but I understood. I was suddenly overwhelmed and began to cry little warm tears. I was a stranger to them but felt profoundly loved. This was a special kind of love and acceptance that I had not felt in a long time, and I did not want that blessing to ever end. The warmth of Timothy's hand welcomed me not only to his family, but back to my relationship with God. I felt loved, as Timothy and Gail love their own daughters, and I also felt blessed and welcomed as a child of God.

17

This Shabbat blessing of the children has shaped my faith. I've spent countless Friday dinners with various Jewish mothers and fathers who blessed my head as I befriended their children. They protected me from harm and nourished my spirit. They welcomed me into their home when I needed love the most; they healed me with their hands and with their words.

This presence of the Holy Spirit in the peace of Shabbat filled me with love that sustained me. I knew I wanted to reconnect with my Catholic faith in college, and raise a family of faith like these inspiring parents had. I am being confirmed in the spring, and my Jewish friends are just as loving and supportive now as they were when I needed them most, five years ago. I am so blessed to be one of God's children among them. Shabbat Shalom!

The Spirit Whispered: I love you, I have not left you, and I will never leave you. When you are lost, I will find you, and when you need me, I will hold you.

Prayer: Divine Spirit, find me when I am lost. Comfort me, and love me. Calm my soul in the midst of chaos. Restore my faith; heal my heart with your hands. Bless the friends and the families around me who support me and fill me with your love.

Elizabeth Brajevich, *Environmental Economics and Policy; Human Development and Family Studies*
Los Angeles, CA

Whisper Seven: Home is Where the Lord Is

My immigrant parents raised me in a small town outside of Ann Arbor, Michigan. The population of this small town of Saline is not the most diverse and as one may guess, there are difficulties that come along when you, as an outsider, are living in a homogeneous community. There is the fear of discrimination and of not fitting in. The thought of losing your heritage and culture and how your children and their children retain their roots are also worries. Fortunately, through the Holy Spirit, those burdens were lifted.

My family has been a part of the St. Andrew Catholic Church in Saline, Michigan since the early 1990s, and since then my family has been the only Vietnamese family to be members of the parish. The parish has been more than wonderful and welcoming. My parents because of the warm atmosphere, have made St. Andrew's their permanent church.) St. Andrew's is significant for my family in a plethora of ways. First of all, it became a home to my family where we could show our true selves. In this environment, prejudice and stereotypes were eliminated. Everyone saw us for who we really are, which is a crucial factor for anyone who feels different.

Secondly, it became the pivotal institution where my siblings and I learned about our faith. Without catechism and youth groups, my faith would not have been nourished. To be honest, back then I dreaded going to youth group, but in hindsight all those hours spent learning about the teachings of the church paid spiritual dividends in my life. My relationship with God today would not have been the same if it were not for my parish. St. Andrew's brought great things to my family but there is one guaranteed thing that it could not have brought us—our culture.

Growing up, my family often traveled to visit relatives and friends out of state. We would spend time with each other, catch up, and get away from non-Vietnamese people to see our Vietnamese community. As a result of this, my parents would end up taking my siblings and me to Vietnamese Masses. Obviously, they took us because going on Sundays was obligatory, but they also took us to teach us about Vietnamese culture and how Catholicism varied back in the homeland. Aside from visiting loved ones to keep in touch with our culture, a tradition that my family has is our annual pilgrimage to Carthage, Missouri.

Each summer, during the first week of August, we pack our camping gear and make our journey down south to celebrate the Marian Days. The Marian Days, or Đại Hội Thánh Mẫu, are held by The Congregation of the Mother Co-Redemptrix, a Catholic institute for Vietnamese who have chosen religious life. Each year, tens of thousands of people gather from around the country to celebrate Mother Mary, particularly the feast of her Assumption. A weekend of festivities takes place! Activities include karaoke, eating delicious food, Mass (which is held outside every evening), and most important of all, learning about our faith and how to apply it to the real world. Here, meeting new people is effortless. Everyone essentially has the same interests and commonalties, which are being Vietnamese, Catholic, and knowing how to have a great time. These encounters often times become life-long friendships.

Regardless of living in a predominately non-Vietnamese community, the imprint of my parents' heritage and culture reside with my siblings and me. From the day we were brought into this world, they have passed down many important things to us, from their native tongue to the most important of all, faith. I believe God has plans for every little thing; out of all places in the country, my parents chose to live in Saline. Although I am not certain of what that plan has in store, our family found a wonderful community, and there we manage to balance and meld two cultures together.

The Spirit Whispered: You have nothing to fear, for there is always a plan. With God, no matter where you go, there will always be a community where you can find care and support.

Prayer: Divine Spirit, come and touch the hearts of those who hold prejudice. Let their minds be open and comfort those who feel estranged. Protect and give hope to those who have been treated unfairly. Bless those who face discrimination, for you love us all equally.

Quyen Hoang, *Comparative Cultures and Politics*
Saline, MI

"Facing daily challenges with a prayer,
for the grace of an open mind,
an informed conscience and courage to act accordingly,
is a fail-safe path, no matter the outcome."

Samuel J. Thomas, Ph.D.
Professor Emeritus
Department of History
Michigan State University

Whisper Eight: Finding Courage

I was just a little girl who was alone and afraid. I walked through the school hallways tightly clutching my books to my chest. I barely ate and I only went to school when I was too weak to put up a good fight. I knew this wasn't who I was but there was a deep-rooted fear of life within me that was constantly weighing me down. I sat in my room and cried because at the age of thirteen, I was already afraid that no one would love me because of all of my fears; and because I didn't believe anyone else could love me, I forgot to love myself. When I looked at my pale, thin face in the mirror, I could see the life withdrawn from my eyes. I didn't know who had taken it, but I really wanted it back. I was so distracted by what I thought were flaws in myself that I forgot to look around and see all of the people who were right there by my side, including God. Some days I just wanted to lie down in the snow and dissolve, sinking deep into the core of the earth so I wouldn't have to walk another day on it. Little did I know, every day that I woke up, God was giving me strength for another day. Every time I worked up the confidence to walk through the school doors and face another eight hours of shame, I won another battle against my anxiety and with each battle, I grew.

In middle school I was blessed with feelings and emotions that I just did not know how to process at such a young age. I saw people hurting and it hurt me. I saw people who were sick and it made me feel sick. I took the weight of the world upon my shoulders and felt every burden carried by the people around me. As I grew, I became better at processing those feelings. Although there is so much pain and conflict, there is so much beauty. The Spirit took me down a long and winding path to get me to where I am today. The Spirit led me through times of trouble and despair so that I would be capable of feeling joy to the same degree I used to feel pain. I am so thankful for days of worry-free laughter because there was a day when I didn't have that. I wouldn't have the appreciation for the world around me if I hadn't had such big fears to overcome.

Some may see me as emotional or sensitive but now I know that I was just born to feel. Through this journey, I have found the one thing I am most passionate in life about and that is life itself. I am in love with the earth because it's God's truest creation. It doesn't lie or steal or beg or deceive. It is molded by our own two hands but at the end of the day, the sun still sets, the moon still appears, and God still reigns. I am in love with animals for their ability to connect with us. The impact they can have on a human life is truly inspiring. I have never felt closer to God than I do when standing face to face with my horse or watching him run through the pasture. It's hard to tell these days what is artificial and what is real, but it is impossible to fake the sound of a hoof beating the solid earth like God's very own drum.

The Spirit whispers to me on the winds that blow through my horse's mane; the winds that ignite the wheat fields into their pre-harvest dance; the winds that encourage an applause amongst the trees. I may struggle finding a place to belong among people but God has led me to beautiful places and incredible creatures that make my life something spectacular. Through my faith and my trust in the Spirit, I have broken the shackles that once bound me so tightly and I found a freedom that has allowed me to courageously chase my dreams. That scared little girl will always be inside of me, and some days it's still really tough. But now I know, no matter how lonely I may feel, I have God beside me – an incredible, unstoppable, underestimated force.

The Spirit Whispered: You are stronger than you realize. Dig deep into your soul and trust in me. I know you can rise above your fear. I will never leave you alone, so lean on me in times of trouble

Prayer: Divine Spirit, open my heart and lead me to you when anxiety burns within me. Help me to realize the emptiness in worrying about the things I cannot change and peace when I turn to you. Pull me close and free me from fear.

Kayla Keyser, *Animal Science*
Midland, MI

Whisper Nine: Imperfectly Perfect

A lot of life is looking to the next step. When I get to high school, when I graduate and when I have a job. It's easy to get caught up in the planning and organizing, trying to get every detail perfect. I found myself anxious about the future, frantically trying to fit my life into a planner and work out every moment of my day so that all would go according to my plan of what life should be, of what I should be. I wanted to be the pretty, popular girl, the one who was loved by everyone, always smiling and surrounded by friends. The girl who got straight A's and never had to try, the one who made varsity on every sports team and could draw beautifully with her eyes closed.

But of course, no one is perfect. I was trying to push myself into this mold of the perfect girl, when in reality that picture I had in my head was far from perfect, and the more I tried, the worse I felt. It got to the point where I didn't even know who I was anymore. I continued to push people away, because if they got too close, they might see through the mask I was wearing. I never wanted to ask for help, because perfect people never have problems, and if they did, they could fix everything on their own. I had trapped myself and I couldn't find a way out.

One night in March of my sophomore year of high school, I couldn't sleep. It was around 2:30 in the morning when I got a message from one of my friends. I knew she was going through a hard time in her life, but nothing could have prepared me for what I saw on the screen. She told me she wanted to die; that her life just wasn't worth it anymore, and she was so tired of all of the pain and the loneliness. It seemed to her like there was no other way out, and that it would be best for everyone if she wasn't there to burden them.

I stared at the words for a long time. All I could think was "Why me? I'm terrible at this stuff, and I don't want to mess this up." I wished I could push it aside and put on a smile, like I did with everything else that made me appear less than perfect in my life. I didn't want to help her, but I also knew that I had to. So I did the only thing I could think of, something that I hadn't done in a long time: I prayed.

"Okay God, You put me here. I don't understand why you picked me for this, but I... I really need your help right now. Tell me what you want me to say to her."

I started typing a response back to my friend, and it was as though the words flew into my head. I could barely write fast enough to keep up.

"Life is imperfect. Life is filled with ups and downs, but if you don't have hope, you'll never make it past the low points. Although you might not see it, you are worth so much more than you could ever imagine. Your life may seem like it is impossible, like there is no way you can ever be happy, but you have to trust me. You are so incredibly loved, and I am always here for you. It feels like everything is too broken to fix, but those broken pieces can be made into something beautiful."

We talked for a few hours, but it wasn't until after I had made sure that she was going to be okay that I realized what I had said. The words I wrote weren't just meant for her, they were for me, too.

I had been so focused on becoming this perfect girl that I had created in my mind, and I'd forgotten that God's idea of a perfect me is very different. God doesn't want me to be someone I'm not. He created me to be me; to love the gifts and the imperfections that he gave me, because those things are what make me, me.

It's not like that day was the end, and that ever since then my life has been only ups, because no one's life is. I still struggle with insecurity, and I still find myself trying to be perfect and hide my flaws. When I do, I remember that my imperfections are what makes me perfect in God's eye and his love for me is what makes me beautiful.

The Spirit Whispered: Stop striving to be perfect. I made you out of love, and I love you for who you are unconditionally.

Prayer: Divine Spirit, help us to remember your unconditional love for us. Help us to see that you created each of us as a unique person, with our imperfections. We ask that you give us the opportunity to share your love with others, to help them to see that they are beautiful because they are your creations.

Marilyn Werner, *Microbiology*
Okemos, MI

Two rules to live by:
"Don't do anything you wouldn't
want to tell your mother.
Character is what you do
when no one is watching."

Andrea Larkin
District Court Judge
East Lansing, MI

Whisper Ten: "Do You Love Me?"

The summer after my high school graduation I expected to feel on top of the world. Instead, it felt like my life was spinning out of control. I was scared about the future, sad about saying goodbye to friends, and struggling to repair my broken heart. I tried to take my problems to God, but unlike the past where I was comforted, this time I received nothing. Life continued spiraling downward until I concluded God was the source of my problems. He wanted me to suffer even though I begged him to lighten the burden. I was purposely ignored.

I attended a Catholic youth conference that summer. It made me feel rejected because I saw my friends thanking God, singing, and smiling. I was disgusted. If I don't feel his presence, then no one else should. I couldn't help thinking:

Why don't I feel happy? I am surrounded by people who love me, yet I feel so alone. Am I wasting my life, believing in someone who doesn't care about me? I am meaningless to God even though I am a good person. I follow the rules, go to church and pray. I teach religious education! What more does he want? Why is he punishing me? I don't deserve this pain.

With the help of my family, I survived the summer and started my first year at Michigan State University. I wrote in my journal: "Great! I can finally get away from everyone who thinks I am a holy person. Maybe I will get a skull tattoo and start drinking. That will show God that I don't care about him anymore either."

The biggest mistake I made those first weeks was dwelling on everything that God was "doing wrong" instead of looking at my blessings. I wanted God, but I was convinced that he was mad at me. I tried everything I could think of to spark that relationship with him again. But nothing could make me feel connected. What stung the most was that I knew he could hear me, but didn't do anything about my prayers. In fact praying was sickening to me, it was a reminder of how alone I really was.

"God, why can't I find happiness in what used to make me happy? It's my eighteenth birthday today. All I wanted was to feel loved by you and to feel joy in life, but instead I am crying alone in my bed."

My parents wanted me to drop out of college because they saw how miserable I was. In particular, I remember one evening where I overheard my roommates making fun of me because I go to church. Their words stung and I just wanted to cry but ended up going to dinner with them because I had no one else.

I tried to hide everything and put on a smile, but the pain became too much to conceal. A few of my friends reached out to me, but nothing they said made me feel any better. This desolation was something I had to face myself. No one understood. Not even the priests in the confessional or my best friends back home. I decided it was time for me to take action and signed up for a retreat at the student parish.

On retreat, I was overcome with the need to talk to a guy sitting at a nearby table. The Holy Spirit was hinting that he had wisdom to share. So I walked by and oddly enough he started a conversation. I told him a little about the issues I had been going through and when I finished he stood up and asked me to go for a walk with him. He explained how he went through similar experiences and gave me some advice. He told me not to give up. That desolation refines your love for God, just like gold is refined in fire. Finally! Someone understands what it's like to go through this internal torture.

A few weeks later, I met up with him again to see how things were going. He asked if anything was better, almost as if he expected a change. I was still just as frustrated as I had been since June. I worried that I might end up like this for the rest of my life, and was convinced that I was going to be the grumpiest old person ever.

That night, I was awakened by bright lights and funny noises. I thought it was my roommate making funny noises. Looking back, I realized that God wanted to talk to me. I huffed out of my room and went for a walk in the basement of my dorm. Sulking around in the shadows with my blanket, I eventually fell onto my knees crying and cursing out God. Looking at the Crucifix on my rosary I wondered if this was some kind of sick joke. This whole God thing is ridiculous. "God, this is the breaking point, you have pushed me too far. I give up." Exhausted, I sat there, my face in the dust and cried.

The next morning, I slept though my alarm and missed my first class. I woke up as an exam in my second class was starting. Lurching out of bed, sweaty with crusted tears, I hopped on my bike.

"Really God? Really? After I spent all that time last night talking to you, the least you could have done for me would have been wake me up on time."

Slush was pelting my face, my fingers were frozen, and my hair was in a huge knot. Never in my life have I felt SO pathetic. And it was at that moment that God decided to reach out to me. All He said was, "Anna, do you still love me?" I wanted to snap back, but I hesitated.

I was reminded of the bible verse where Jesus asks Peter if he loves him. God had been testing me. I decided I didn't care if he ever returned my love, because I needed him. This experience of loneliness has changed me. I can't explain how, but something is different inside of me. I threw my hands up in the air (almost falling off my bike) and I sang, "Praise the Lord", with all my heart as I biked down the river trail, blessing everyone I passed. I didn't care about making a scene, because God was with ME.

This entire experience was part of your plan, and it wasn't a curse or punishment. It was a gift, to experience a deeper appreciation and respect for you. But more specifically, you have a special love for me, and I am the only person who can love you the way I do. It got to the point where you wanted me to mean nothing or to mean everything to you. – *November 1st (All Saint's Day)*

My problems are not solved nor do I feel particularly connected to God, but I know that he is up to something. He knows what he is doing and he is waiting for the day when he can reveal his secrets to me.

The Spirit Whispered: Everyone can love God when life is good. Accept the suffering as a gift.

Prayer: Divine Spirit, help me to see ways in my life that I can suffer gracefully. Thank you for the opportunity to share in the cross of Jesus Christ.

Anna Fedoronko, *Human Biology*
Saline, MI

Whisper Eleven: My Gift to You

There is a time in every girl's life when she feels some kind of insecurity. I suppose my time started my sophomore year of high school. I had seen many of my friends with boyfriends and I felt like no one even glanced my way. Some days it didn't bother me, but others I would lay in bed tormented by my thoughts. Why did no one like me? Was I not pretty enough? Was I that weird? Was I too much of a "Goody-Two Shoes?" Was I unlovable? That last thought taunted me especially.

Don't get me wrong. I knew my family and friends loved and accepted me, but to me, there was a difference between being loved by people who have known you most of your life and being loved by someone who chose to get to know you. It was tough at times, so I put on a mask. To anyone who asked, I was fine. My life was great. On the inside, though, was a different story, so I started praying.

I prayed for God to help me realize and believe that I am loved. I also prayed to know that I was *worth* being loved. In His own time, and in his own way, God answered. I started dating my current boyfriend, John, at the end of my junior year of high school, but my story doesn't end there.

Having a boyfriend didn't mean that all my doubts and insecurities immediately disappeared. Sure, now I had someone who told me that I was beautiful and that I was loved, but I struggled to believe it. John seemed to assume it was just modesty that made me shy away from compliments, but it wasn't. I couldn't believe the words, as much as I wanted to, because I was still struggling to know if it was true or not. Was I really lovable?

My doubts only increased the more time went on. It came to the point that I began to feel selfish every time I was with John. I felt as though I was "forcing" him to love me and I often worried that I was taking him away from something – or someone – better. What if John and I weren't supposed to be together? What if there was another woman out there who John was supposed to be with? Was I being too selfish?

Part of my doubts came from a lack of trust in God and His love for me. I wanted to fill that desire for love in my life, but I didn't trust that God would love me despite my sins and failings. Yes, I claimed that I trusted in God, but did I give him every part of me? Not even slightly. I held on to the tentative control I thought I had on my life, basically rejecting God before he could reject me.

After several long months of going back and forth on this, I began going to Mass twice a week and Adoration on Tuesday nights. I spent some time praying in Adoration and I kept thinking about all those things that I'd been agonizing over in the past few months. Finally, I laid it all before God and asked, "God, is this relationship right for me? I feel so selfish, like maybe I'm taking John away from who he really should be with."

I heard the Spirit whisper, "Who put John in your life? You didn't take him. He is my gift to you. Just like my love, you can't selfishly take what you've been freely given."

It dawned on me, I wasn't being selfish, I was just afraid to accept the love that God had put in my life. Every day I try to accept just a little more of God's love, and each day I come that much closer to living the life God wants for me, a life filled with love.

The Spirit Whispered: I put people in your life who will bring out the best in you. I freely give you my love and it is not selfish to accept what I give you.

Prayer: Divine Spirit, fill us with your courage to both accept that we are loved and embrace the gifts we've been given. Help us to remember that you love us despite our failings. Grant us the courage to turn to you when we need you most.

Rebecca Jean Barta, *Athletic Training*
Stevensville, MI

Whisper Twelve: Faith

My story begins my freshmen year of college. I was attending a community college and was living with my grandfather at the time. This was an interesting time in my life because, although I had gone through the Catholic school system, I was now attending a non-faith based college. It was during this period when I began to learn more about my faith through my grandpa. Along with his teaching me the word of God, and relating it to our world today, Jesus had revealed himself to people at our local middle school in an astonishing way! During adoration, which a group of fourth graders were attending in the school's chapel, God chose to reveal himself by showing His face upon the host that was resting inside the monstrance. News spread quickly throughout our community, and because my sisters were attending the middle school, the reality of it hit me quite hard.

Just a short while after the initial shock of this miracle began to wear off, I was blessed with being able to speak with a good friend's mother. She had personally gone and seen the beautifully imprinted host, and told me all about the people's amazement as well as their joyful tears. This was the eye opener that had led me to desire more truth about God, and while it took some time to click, I started to understand that the best place to get that life-giving truth was the bible. This time brought me close to the Holy Spirit because I was able to talk to the Consoler, and hear where he was leading me. I began to ask for more and more direction, and thankfully my heart was opened to grace.

One night, while staying at my grandpa's, he and a friend were talking about the Holy Spirit. This was a bit intense conversation because they are from different denominations. I could tell that the topic meant a lot to both of them. So, I said a little prayer to God asking for guidance. Then I sat with them and listened. At the right time, I saw an opportunity to weave together a path of understanding between these two men. It was as if they were both saying the same thing only in a different tongue and each one was just having trouble hearing the other's words. The topic was how people receive the Holy Spirit, and humbly through the Holy Spirit, I believe the answer was given to my heart. Everyone being made by God and suffered for by Jesus Christ during his passion is capable and able to receive "The Gift of the Father!" The way to do this is by making a childlike act of faith by receiving Jesus as your Savior. The truth is that every person can ask the Holy Spirit for help and God may fill their heart, but initially people must have the faith to ask. As Jesus tells us in scripture, "Ask and you shall receive, seek and you shall find, knock and the door will be opened unto you!"

The night before my uncle was scheduled to go into heart surgery, I was praying fervently for God to be with him and protect him during his surgery. I was also going through a very intense examination of conscience and preparing myself to ask Jesus for forgiveness. As I said my night prayers, I almost fell asleep when I heard a voice. It spoke to me and told me to finish my prayers. When I finally finished my prayers, I immediately was given a vision of a white butterfly. Confused, I opened and refocused my eyes before closing them again. The second time I closed my eyes, I saw another vision of the Blessed Virgin Mary. At that point I said to her, "I am listening." Although it took time for the message to come through clearly, I truly believe that Mother Mary was drawing me closer to Jesus. The message was, "Heaven is for real, and Jesus will take you to heaven. For God is the way, the truth, and the life and no one comes to the Father except through HIM!"

The Spirit Whispered: You are to walk by faith and not by sight. Blessed are those who believe and have not seen.

Prayer: Divine Spirit, thank you for the love that you have given to me. I pray that I may always remain steadfast in faith, and humble in heart. May your consolations live in my mind today and forever.

Nathan R.T. Penn, *Agribusiness Management*
Jackson, MI

Whisper Thirteen: The Angel and the Pen

I sat in the front of the classroom on my first day of the Women's Studies class. The front seats made the room appear more intimate and welcoming. My professor was amicable and was as eager to teach the material as I was to learn it. Our first reading was from Bell Hook's, "Feminism is for Everybody," which offered a promising confrontation for my seemingly conflicting beliefs of Catholicism and feminism. I stumbled after coming upon the sentence, "She cannot be anti-abortion and an advocate of feminism."

I paused.

The ridged dichotomy split my mind in two, and seemed to provide no space for Catholic-defined morality in women's studies. I couldn't believe that these views could be so black-and white, and knew that others must surely find Hook's avowal unreasonable. I vehemently attempted to combat Hook's statement in class, only to be met with smirks and further opposition from my classmates. It seemed that each feminist author denounced the practice of religion's antithesis, to women's liberation. I yearned for a crutch, a safe-haven to discover a balance between my feuding worlds.

I prayed every day before class. I prayed for the strength not to be complacent, not to solely speak through my voice, but to let the voice of the Spirit be heard in my arguments and to glean a sliver of mutual understanding. Like attempting to cut a diamond with glass, I began to carve and intertwine my views alongside those of the critical theorists. My classmates, as well as many feminist theorists, deprecated the church without fully understanding its teachings, and I had the drive to prove that there was a place in which the two could intersect. The two were perpendicular, not parallel. That was the problem: Women's Studies viewed the church and feminist politics to be two lines, infinitely moving in the same direction yet never finding a moment of juncture, when the meeting of the intervals was inherently inevitable. It was impossible for me to leave behind a crucial piece of my religious identity and surrender it to illegitimate feminist sources. I researched, analyzed, theorized, and wrote about religion's relationship to feminism to prove that my faith, my beliefs, and that I myself had a place in Women's Studies.

It was the Spirit who guided me. The Spirit allowed me to continue to write and defend my faith. I recalled the beatitude: Blessed are those who are ridiculed due to the name of Jesus Christ for they will see the kingdom of heaven. In that I found strength. I wasn't the most popular voice in my Women's Studies class, but I was a prominent one. With the help of the Spirit I told my own story and found the courage to make the Spirit's influence visible on paper.

The Spirit Whispered: Have patience and hope; I will guide you in your call to evangelize.

Prayer: Divine Spirit, let us mirror your divinity in our lives. Be near us in times of trial, and make porous our hearts to absorb your glorified essence. Move us to utilize our gifts to do your will, and give us the strength to share your love in hopes of reaching those who do not know you.

Lauren Genevieve Straley, *English*
Flushing, MI

Whisper Fourteen: Be Still and Know That I Am God

I was lying face down on the floor, hands folded, praying in a prostrate position. I felt as though my whole mind and soul were reaching up toward heaven, searching for an answer to my discernment question. I prayed that God would open my ears that I would hear God's will for my vocation and career path, listening with all my might. As my mind was reaching far, far out, the Spirit whispered to me, "Be still and know that I am God."

I know for sure this voice was not just my imagination, but it was truly God speaking to me because my heart and soul were immediately filled with such joy as tears ran down my cheeks, and I looked up to heaven. Words were not needed to thank God for this gift because my soul radiated my thanks. That moment seems almost indescribable, especially since I have never been very eloquent with words, but that was part of its beauty because God was not asking me to speak, but to just be still. I laid prostrated in God's presence with such joy, that I never wanted to get up or move, but only to lay there for hours with my Father, my friend and Savior. I know in time God will reveal to me what I am to do with my life, all I have to do is trust.

The Spirit Whispered: Be patient, and trust in me. As it says in Proverbs, "Commit your work to the Lord, and your plans will be established." The Father's will may not be revealed as soon as you would like, so pray for guidance every day, and do all that you do for me. Trust, and you will receive the strength and courage you need for the building up of my kingdom.

Prayer: Divine Spirit, please help me to trust you completely. Help me to commit each and every day to you, and see your face in all people. Help me remember that I do not need to constantly speak during prayer, but just listen and be still in your presence.

Brianne Feldpausch, *Human Biology*
St. Johns, MI

The true relationships you form with your peers,
your professors and administrators at
Michigan State
will last you a lifetime.
Look and find a sense of commitment,
communication of values
and an overall sense of trust in each other and
your drive towards success will become complete.

Mark Dantonio
Michigan State University Football Coach

Whisper Fifteen: Out of the Darkness:
My Struggle with Epilepsy

Ambulances, the sound of the sirens, the EMTs all rushing, not knowing where I was: this all happens with my serious medical condition. I am an epileptic. Epilepsy is described by many as a seizure disorder. My life and death experiences because of epilepsy have not only affected me, but also the people around me.

My seizures began when I was just ten months old and since then have gotten progressively worse. Though many people describe it as a seizure disorder, there is so much more to it than that. It is a neurological disorder. When people say that they have epilepsy, it means the neurons or clusters of nerve cells in their brains signal abnormally. When the neurons in the brain are disturbed, it can cause a number of different things including unusual behavior, unconsciousness, muscle spasms and much more. Types of epilepsy include absence, Temporal Lobe, Neocortical and others.

Epilepsy has affected many everyday areas of my life. For example, it is very important to establish good sleeping habits as the medication itself can make me sleepy. If I don't take the medication at the correct intervals it can be dangerous and cause me to seize and interfere with my sleeping habits. Certain medications can cause my appetite to decrease and lead to weight loss. Therefore, it is vital that I eat healthy, smaller meals throughout the day. The amount of medication I am on impacts my activities. I experience delayed reactions and slower speech, so I am not able to communicate with others as easily. Depending on how severe the seizure is, I could miss a few days or possibly weeks of school. In any event, any of these situations could cause me to get behind in my studies.

My condition has impacted not only my life, but the lives of my family, friends and teachers. I have a serious case of epilepsy. I can drop and have a seizure anytime anywhere. A few examples of where it has happened to me are in the grocery store, at school, in dance class, at Rite Aid and at my track meet. Since I don't have any warning signs of when or where a seizure is going to happen, the people around me have to be prepared. One year it was so bad that

I was in and out of the hospital the whole year. I even fell flat on my face once hitting the cement, knocking out one tooth, chipping another one, and scratching up my face. All of my teachers have been made aware of my condition.

Everyone in my immediate circle is involved in some way. My sisters were in charge of packing an overnight bag and getting all my medications together, while my brother was in charge of flagging down the ambulance. Over the years, I know that it has made my siblings very nervous, especially my youngest sister, Ireland. Even today after I have been seizure free for two years, Ireland asks me almost daily if I am okay and if I have taken my pills. Finally, in the past six months she no longer fears being alone with me. Our close neighbors have always been there for support as have my relatives. I think it was difficult on my friends, as they did not know how to handle it. The Spirit whispered to me that I would be ok and not to worry but to trust that I will be taken care of. So I began trusting that God was in control and God would help me deal with this as long as I trust in him.

Due to numerous hospital stays, I have come in contact with a variety of health professionals including EMTs, emergency room staff, the pediatric unit nurses and doctors, and everyone in the Pediatric Intensive Care Unit. Upon waking from a seizure, I usually find myself on the floor. I have always taken comfort in the kind faces of the many EMTs, as their professionalism and compassion have always made me feel that I was in good hands. The staff in the Emergency Room have always been attentive and thorough. As soon as I was moved to either the pediatric unit or the PICU, the nurses and doctors made sure to answer all of our questions and treated me with the utmost respect. They have a tough job dealing with so many sick children, yet they do it with such grace. I have come to truly admire those who work in the health profession and because of these experiences, I have been inspired to go into the health field myself.

The challenges I have faced because of my epilepsy have affected not only me, but those around me. As a lifelong epileptic, I feel I have learned that education is key in managing this illness. Knowledge is power. My family, friends, and health professionals have all rallied around me, helping me handle my situation. Although epilepsy is a serious condition, it shouldn't stop anyone from leading and living a purpose filled life.

The Spirit Whispered: Don't give up, you can make it through, don't stop believing in yourself.

Prayer: Divine Spirit please lead and guide me through these tough and complicated times. I know you are guiding my steps, I have faith and will follow the path.

Isabel Bohr, *Therapeutic Recreation*
Okemos, MI

"You go to college to prove yourself
to your family and friends.
You leave college no longer looking to prove
but knowing who you are
and who you are becoming
to make a difference in this world."

Gene Orlando
Tennis Coach at MSU

Whisper Sixteen: The Dome That Consumed Me

A dark dome of negative thoughts consumed me and the light that touched me vanished, leaving me in total darkness. I couldn't tell what the dome was made of; all I knew was that my parents were on the other side laughing joyfully, not knowing that their daughter was over in the dark, scared and alone. I reached out to see what the wall is made of, thinking maybe I could rise over it. But before I could get close, a burning coldness scorched my hand and quickly consumed my whole body. The pain turned me flat on my back. I started howling for someone, anyone to comfort me, but no one came. No one noticed me as I prayed for it to stop. I cracked open my eyes to see that the dome was now crystal clear and had tightened around me, shaping to fit my body. The burning coldness I had experienced before was suddenly all over my body, burning my flesh but at the same time freezing my insides. I was frozen, unable to speak, just standing and feeling.

My consciousness started to drift off. Why was this happening to me? Everyone around me was content, going on in their lives, not suffering like me. Was it me? What had I done to deserve this? What was wrong with me? Did I deserve to be happy at all? Did I even deserve to live?

I spent months like this, tangled in my monstrous thoughts, never knowing when it would end. Wishing it could just stop, wishing for anything to put me out of my misery. Then something brought me back to reality: my mother asking if everything was okay. "The usual, nothing different," I said without thinking. "Everything's fine." I had been lying to her for months, maybe even years. I rarely looked her in the eye, but this was – I thought – my last opportunity to do so. I looked into her eyes and saw something alien to me. Happiness? Comfort? Joy? No, something stronger, something so strong, so powerful, I recognized the one thing that I thought I would never see again. Hope.

"Mom," I mumbled almost silently.

"Yes, honey?" She responded.

I took a short quick breath and was almost certain my heart had hesitated in its rhythm. It took all my strength just to say her name. Now, I had to quickly gather my courage back as my mother waited for me to answer. I knew I had to tell her - tell her that my skin was boiling as I stood there. But once I spoke it aloud I could never take it back, I could never go back. The result was unpredictable; my body froze at the realization. If I said what was on my mind, my life could be destroyed. I could be left completely alone to defend myself, and that's exactly what had stopped me all the times before. But this time, my heart knew that the chance of being accepted, that *hope*, was much greater than being destroyed. I was already being ripped apart limb by limb. Why not take a chance?

I breathed in and out slowly, summoned all of my courage and said, "Mom... I want to end it all."

I told my mom what was going on inside me. When I was done, I looked at her and waited for her response.

She hugged me and gripped me close. I went limp as a tear crawled down my cheek. The next thing I knew both my mother and I were sobbing. Little did I know that my mom had gone through the same thing, like her sister and her father before her. It was genetics, she said. But I called it a curse. I was just glad to know that I was not alone, that I could change my life, move on to greater things, be greater than what I was in that moment.

Slowly but surely, I sought help. I expressed, I confessed, I did anything I could to move on.

Telling my mom about my depression was not the point when the burning cold stopped. Even now it remains, reminding me of what I felt once, what I still feel. All I know is that in that moment when I told my mom a little part of the burning died down, and cracks began to appear in my impenetrable dome. It was the first step in breaking free.

The Spirit Whispered: You are never alone, you always have hope, and you always have love, you always have me.

Prayer: Divine Spirit, I pray that anyone who has struggled with darkness and has felt consumed by it realize that you are there for them. That they have you, and you bring them hope, love and support in their darkest times. I ask you to help them realize that they are not dealing with their struggles alone, that you are with them.

Karoline Knedgen, *Human Biology*
Novi, MI

"To be successful, you have to
get up every morning with determination,
if you are going to go to bed with satisfaction."

Suzy Merchant
Women's Basketball Coach at MSU

Whisper Seventeen: InspiRING

The two crystal butterflies on my silver ring glisten gorgeously in the sunlight as I shift my hand back and forth ever so slightly. The complexity of the crystal cut makes the ring sparkle in such a magnificent way that its beauty captivates my attention and calms me. I remember when my mom presented me with the ring. She gave it to me as an early graduation present during my senior year spring break. The first thing I thought was: butterflies. Butterflies are known to symbolize a plethora of things such as beauty, change, hope, freedom, faith, and purity. Whenever I see two butterflies flying side by side it sparks a connection to my deceased grandparents and their love. The gift is so much more to me than what most might think. It is a reminder of my grandparents whose love has always inspired me.

My grandparents were happily married for sixty-five years before they passed. They were best friends and must have been great parents (based on their wonderful product of a woman that I am proud to call my mother). My grandma was probably the cutest little old lady who ever lived. She was just under five feet. Everyone in my family had to crouch down to hug her. She was a strong and clever woman who made the most delicious Polish food. As my grandmother grew older she was diagnosed with a series of medical problems, one of which was dementia. My grandma slowly became forgetful of things she once knew. It was hard for me and my family to witness her failure to recognize us, even worse, her husband. My grandpa stood by her side and took care of her through it all. He developed and carried out a strict routine week after week to keep things as familiar as possible for her. He did an exceptional job of caring for my grandmother and aiding her in daily activities. When the job became too daunting for my grandpa to handle alone, he admitted her to hospice.

I sensed that it was close to the end of my grandma's life when I went to visit her at Faith Hospice Center. I saw my grandma lying in bed tucked under a baby blue blanket. My grandpa who was beside my grandma's bed, greeted me with a weak hug. He resumed his position sitting down holding her hand under the blanket and ever so gently stroked her smooth pale face. I was silent. I was afraid to come any closer to her bedside. My grandpa whispered to my grandma, "Helen, Katie is here...Helen, come on now, open those beautiful blue eyes of yours and say hello to your granddaughter." She didn't even flinch. I fought back tears as my grandpa kept attempting to wake her. "Let her rest Grandpa." I reached out and held her hand. She was 90 years old and had lived a great life. I prayed to God that her suffering would end and God would take her to a better place.

Every one of her children and grandchildren came to visit her during her last couple days. My immediate family, grandpa, a few relatives, and I were all gathered in my grandma's room when she took her last breath. We were laughing and sharing old memories to distract us. My mom informed us that my grandma was almost gone. Silence filled the room. We were all frozen, waiting for the inevitable. One of the hospice nurses came in to inform us that she had left us. I looked at my grandpa softly weeping and felt my heart sink into my stomach. My vision became blurred by tears. She passed away on Tuesday, June 14, 2011. Never before had I lost someone so dear to my heart. The shock was numbing.

Less than three weeks later, on my birthday, July 8th, my grandpa passed away. He went to Florida to watch the last space shuttle launch with my uncle. Two minutes after take-off he tripped and fell going up steps. The fall was so severe that it took his life. His passing was a huge shock to my family. He was always the life of every party cracking jokes and pulling all sorts of shenanigans. He had always been in great physical and mental shape until my grandma's passing. Yet, how can one live with a broken heart? My grandmother was his everything. My family believed he rode that space shuttle up to heaven to be reunited with the one he loved. Although it was hard to attend my grandpa's funeral so soon after losing my grandma, my mom and I were comforted by two yellow butterflies flying high in the sky. Similar to how time would heal our pain of losing my grandparents, time had transformed the once ordinary caterpillars into the majestically fluttering butterflies. God must have set the butterflies' flight to cross our path as a sign to comfort us and show that my grandparents were together in a better place.

My grandpa and grandma's love is my inspiration. Watching my grandpa's commitment to taking care of my grandmother every day with love and understanding inspired me to decide to commit to a profession in which I can implement the same comforts for others as he did for my grandmother. Witnessing someone you love dearly pass away is probably the weirdest feeling anyone could ever experience. At first, I felt a deep sadness, then failure to believe it happened, then a sense of peace, and finally acceptance. Dealing with people passing away every day in one's profession is not an easy thing. Yet, I believe I could do it. If not me, then who? My dream is to become a physician assistant working in hospice or geriatrics. I love elderly people, and I would embrace the opportunity to ensure their comfort as they pass on to a better place.

On the day of my high school graduation, a couple years after my grandparents' death, I could not find my butterfly ring. A sense of panic flooded into my veins as I searched everywhere, and still came up with nothing. I was so ashamed and embarrassed that I had lost the early graduation gift my mom gave me that I didn't ask my mom to help me search for it. Since the ring was all I had left to remind me of my grandparents, I felt like losing it was like losing them all over again. I was upset that I could not wear the butterfly ring for the ceremony. I was devastated that I had misplaced my most prized possession and that my grandparents wouldn't be with me as I walked up to receive my diploma.

Then it was my first full week of classes at Michigan State University. As I walked back to my dorm, I finally felt content with my life. I felt a slight breeze and put my hand in the pocket of my sweater. While I felt the fuzz inside my pocket something small hit my finger. Surprised and slightly confused, I pulled out a small item that sparkled in the sun. A wave of excitement overcame me as I realized the small item was my butterfly ring. I immediately placed it on my finger and let out a deep sigh. The two butterflies, similar to the ones my mom and I had seen flying in unison over my grandpa's funeral, seemed to shine brighter than ever. In that moment, I knew my grandparents were watching over me. In that moment, I knew I was doing the right thing coming to Michigan State University to start my life-long journey of helping others. In that moment, I felt a comfort and love that I want to share.

The Spirit Whispered: Use what you have been blessed with to love and serve the Lord.

Prayer: Divine Spirit, help us to acknowledge your presence in others and within ourselves. Help us to use our gifts and talents to help others.

Katie Theriault, *Biomedical Laboratory Science*
Grand Rapids, MI

Whisper Eighteen: The Spirit Gives Hope

I thought I trusted God until Friday May 24, 2013. This day was like any other for me until my family and I sat down to dinner. My mom had a worried look on her face and I knew something was wrong. She just came right out and said it, "Your dad went to the doctor; he has cancer." At first I didn't know what to think. I knew nothing other than the fact that my dad had cancer. So I just sat there in a daze. I didn't think it was real. I hoped and prayed that this was just a bad dream and soon I would wake up and my dad wouldn't have cancer. But it wasn't. It was real and as a family we were going to have to deal with it.

I was taught growing up to always have a good line of communication with God. I always had a pretty easy time praying, until that night. I was angry and I was hurt. How could God do this to my dad? How could he do this to my family? As more and more people began to find out that my dad was sick, they would tell me to trust that God had everything handled. How was I supposed to trust God if I felt like God had let me down?

As my dad's surgery approached, we all went to confession. As I walked in to talk with the priest I remember thinking that it didn't matter if I went to confession. God knew I was angry with him and he already had a plan and I could not change that. As I sat down and made the sign of the cross, I just burst into tears. The priest gave me a few moments to compose myself, and then I told him my story. I told him how I had always trusted in God, but now I was having a hard time with that because my dad had cancer and I was scared that he was going to die. I was scared he wouldn't be able to walk me down the aisle. I was scared I was going to lose one of my best friends. He asked me if I had told God my fears. I laughed at him and said no. What could my fears being vocalized to God change? I told him that this was my burden not God's, and that is where he stopped me. He asked me what trusting someone looked like. I didn't know how to respond. I told him that trusting someone was being able to give up all of your worry and fear to that person knowing that they have your best interest at heart. I heard myself say it but I didn't believe it. He smiled and said, "Then how do you think you should go about trusting God again?"

I told him I didn't know and he quickly told me, "Mary Margaret, you do know; you just told me. Give all of your burdens, your fears, your worries over to him. He has your best interest at heart and he will take care of you."

It was there in that confessional that I really learned something I thought I knew. I learned how to really trust God. Before my confession was over, the priest gave me my penance. He told me that from now on whatever prayer I say I have to end it with these eight words. GOD I LOVE YOU. GOD I TRUST YOU. I promised I would and walked out with a newfound hope. Over the next couple of days as I did my penance, the more I said those eight words the more I began to believe what I was saying.

By trusting that God knew my burdens, fears, and worries, I began having hope that things would work out not just the way that I wanted them to, but the way that they needed to. From that day on, I placed my full trust in God and his plan and because of that I was able to hope. I was able to hope that my dad would be okay and that hope has stayed with me as my dad is now cancer free. I was able to have hope by becoming truly vulnerable and giving all my worries to God. God took my worries and my fear and gave them back to me in the form of hope and strength. So I challenge you to trust in God because you will find hope.

The Spirit Whispered: Trust in God. You will find hope.

Prayer: Divine Spirit, please give me the strength to continue to trust in God so that I may always find hope.

Mary Margaret Dunneback, *Kinesiology*
Lansing, MI

Whisper Nineteen: A Breath of Fresh Air

God has always been very present in my life. One memory in particular comes to mind. It was when I was six years old.

It was a warm night and all the neighborhood kids decided to play a game of flashlight tag, so of course I joined in the fun. The game lasted about two hours. There was a lot of running and laughing. When I came home that night, I was out of breath. At first I didn't think anything of it since I had been running around all night. However, when I sat down and tried to relax, I found it harder and harder to breathe. I decided to lay down in my bed but the shortness of breath got worse.

It was now two o'clock in the morning and my breathing was bothering me so much that I decided to wake up my dad. He got up and listened to my breathing. It was obvious to him from my wheezing that he needed to take me to the hospital right away. As we were driving to the hospital, my breathing became so restricted that it caused me to throw up. I was finding it harder and harder to breathe and we were only halfway to the hospital. I heard the spirit whisper, "Pray." It was the only thing left to do, so we prayed. My dad and I prayed a rosary together, and somehow I was able to make it through the rest of the car ride.

I was quickly attended to once we arrived at the hospital. They finally diagnosed that I was suffering a severe asthma attack. I stayed at the hospital all night, breathing in medication to open up my lungs. For a couple months after the attack, I had to take two doses of medicine a day through a breathing machine called a nebulizer. Now I am doing fine, thanks to help of the medical profession.

I firmly believe that the Holy Spirit was there with me that night, watching over me, allowing me to survive such a horrible episode.

The Spirit Whispered: Do not be afraid. I am always there to help and protect you.

Prayer: Divine Spirit, guide us, protect us, and keep us in your embrace. Protect us from all danger and turn our fears and tears into joy.

Jackie Guzman, *Arts and Humanities*
Okemos, MI

Whisper Twenty: Called To Love Ourselves as God Loves Us

Recently, a friend of mine posted a picture of the two of us on Facebook. Right away I started to judge my appearance. I compared myself to my friend. I thought that she looked so amazing and I looked horrible. I pulled out some pictures of me from high school and put them side by side with this current picture. I thought, "What happened? How did I let myself turn into this fat, ugly person?" I then turned to Twitter and said how "#Transformation Tuesday" makes me want to go back to high school and tell my insecure self how amazing and beautiful I was. I wanted to go back to those low points in my high school years and tell myself that I had amazing friends and that I was gorgeous and that I had no reason to be sad or depressed.

At this moment in time, I had forgotten that it is what is on the inside that matters! It is who you are as a person that really counts. Luckily, the Spirit was there to remind me of this. The Spirit whispered to me, "I love you the way you are." It was then that I realized God loves me for me! He doesn't care what I look like. He loves me because I am me. He wasn't comparing me to my friend, so why was I? He loves me unconditionally. If God can love me unconditionally, then why can't I love myself unconditionally? No matter what I do in my life, no matter what I look like, I will always be enough for God.

The Spirit Whispered: Kristyn, you are an amazing person who cares for those around you. You are beautiful inside and out. Your outer beauty doesn't define who you are and definitely doesn't determine how much I love you and it shouldn't determine how much you love yourself.

Prayer: Divine Spirit, thank you for making me the person I am today. Help me remember that I am loved, no matter what I say or do. Help me to love others as you love me.

Kristyn Ann Wilhelm, *Athletic Trainer*
Sterling Heights, MI

"Your generation is much more intelligent
than mine…
but perhaps not as wise.
Together we can make the world
a better place."

Mark Hollis
Athletic Director of MSU

Whisper Twenty-One: Imagine

Imagine that you are in a place where mountains are seen in every direction and the misty air envelops the marvels all around. You are surrounded by winding roads, a farm with lush strawberry fields, and a wave of people intermingling as they share their agricultural secrets. It is a world away, yet the happiness that is seen when the indigenous children's faces light up with gratitude is a moment that ignites an indescribable sense of joy. These wonders are within the people of Ecuador, and I too find a similar sense of hope, resilience, and determination in myself from the Holy Spirit. The beginning purpose of this trip for me was to offer service to the small communities of Ecuador, along with the Archdiocese of Detroit's Youth Justice Group. Through this service experience, I realized it was so much more—it was about letting go of the struggles from my past.

I once thought my life was shaped by the struggles of my past. I chose to put myself in environments which were emotionally draining and not life-giving. I was running away from myself but being still with the Holy Spirit. Truly, I am grateful for the dilemmas in my life because they gave me a new outlook on the world. I discovered that by being focused, honest, and present, I encounter the Spirit. Ecuador gave me the freedom to see the truth and the light.

A wonderful memory of my time in Ecuador is about Samai. Samai's eyes glistened; the four-year-old half-indigenous Caguji boy pointed up, said proudly, "The *luna,* the *luna.*" The full moon was not just graceful in the night sky, it reflected happiness within me; the happiness that only a child can bring. I held his tiny hand, and he felt safe with me in a crowd of strangers. I felt accepted, even with what separated us: our ages and our lifestyles. Samai and I spoke different languages and both of us lived on different continents, but right then I felt a connection which was unspoken. I could not be more in the present moment. I felt free and no longer alone. It was not just a global connection; it was a deeply personal connection. I felt that someone relied on me and I forgot about my pain, I felt love. The journey in Ecuador was a life-changing experience that showed me regardless of one's race or any type of adversity, the deepest connection in our world is the human connection. You may be labeled, shamed, or ridiculed but in the deepest moment of despair, if you have the smallest amount of courage to stay focused in love, you will remain triumphant.

The Spirit Whispered: You were once lost but now you are found. The ashes of your past became fertilizer to an expansive future. You stopped looking left or right but found the stillness within. You were quiet until the power was gained. Now that you are restored, I will see you fly.

Prayer: Help me to make time for stillness, time to listen to you speak.

Joseph Leo Kuzminski, *Education/Psychology*
Romeo, MI

Whisper Twenty-Two: Not Alone

I did not like the idea of being alone. I was not ready for this kind of independence. I was still the girl who got homesick when I was away, called my parents every day, and could not make a decision without the help of someone. How in the world was I going to navigate to a foreign country?

The study abroad program was not through my school. I did not know a soul going, which was not a comforting feeling either. In the weeks leading up to my flight to Italy, I went back and forth on a daily basis trying to decide if I should go. "Maybe I should just go back to school instead, it definitely would be easier," I thought to myself. Even family and friends were telling me that maybe it was best if I did not go; maybe I was not ready. But, my heart was not ready to give up so easily. I felt a pull to go, despite the consensus of people telling me I shouldn't. "You can't come home if you go," they said. I was afraid, but I did not want to let fear stop me. I knew what I had to do.

A few days before I left for Florence, I received a package from a friend. In the package was a small wooden box and inside was a map of Italy and these words: "Have I not commanded you? Be strong and courageous. Do not be afraid; do not be discouraged; for the Lord your God will be with you wherever you go." Joshua 1:9. A feeling of calm washed over me as I read these words and I felt my eyes tear up. I would not be alone on this adventure. God would be with me.

My time in Florence was a time in my life where I felt closest to God. I left on that plane knowing that I would not be alone, and I was not. Wandering the streets of Italy, I felt in my heart a sense of peace and the knowledge that I was not alone, God was with me.

The Spirit Whispered: My beloved child, you are not going on this adventure alone. I am with you and will never leave you. Do not be afraid because I will give you strength every day.

Prayer: Divine Spirit, help me to remember that I am not alone. Help me to remember that wherever life takes me, you will be with me. Help me to not be afraid of the unknown, but to trust God in all circumstances.

Stephanie Lynn Hayley Lazar, *Psychology*
Chicago, IL

Whisper Twenty-Three: The Power of Prayer

Endure this recurring dream. I race through my grandparents' house, a wolf in chase, kind of a twist on Little Red Riding Hood. In the dream, I can always hear my mom and grandma talking in the next room. If I get to them, the wolf won't be able to get me. I'll sprint into that room, only to see that Mom and Grandma moved on to the next room. It's this endless pursuit throughout the house until the wolf finally corners me and I'm forced to wake up.

But one time, as I dashed through the kitchen, I stopped in my tracks. I suddenly grasped that everything was a dream, Mom and Grandma in the next room and the phony wolf behind me. My Grandpa Bud, who had died two years before, sat in a wooden kitchen chair. I *knew* he shouldn't have been there. I knew he wasn't alive. But I was hit with the realization that he and I were real, and that everything surrounding us wasn't.

In my dream, I couldn't breathe, and my pulse went haywire. Grandpa Bud stood up, and I ran into his arms and let them engulf me. I started sobbing uncontrollably. I couldn't believe I had the incredible chance to hug Grandpa Bud again. I looked up; the grin on his face stretched a mile wide. I noticed an incongruous detail. "Grandpa, where are your wrinkles?" His grin widened. My eyes opened even further in disbelief. "Grandpa, where are your glasses?" He replied, "I don't need them anymore, Princess."

Upon waking, I discovered my tears not only on my face but my pillow was soaking wet. It was all just a dream. I cried for over an hour, the rare combination of pure happiness and grief. Finally, I got out of bed and slid open my picture drawer. I scrolled through the pictures and selected every single one with Grandpa Bud.

The pictures brought back memories. A particular Sunday morning came to mind. Grandpa Bud was in critical condition. The doctors didn't think he would wake up. Upsettingly, my mom left for the hospital without me, insisting I still go to religion class. Our family was gathering at the hospital, and it felt wrong for me not to be there. My uncle offered to drive me there after religion class.

I started repeating over and over in my head, "Dear Holy Spirit, please wait until I can say goodbye." I can't emphasize enough the significance this simple phrase held. I knew Grandpa wouldn't ever see or speak to me again, but I wanted to see him before he died. The phrase repeated in my head all the way to class. Upon entering class, I learned we were devoting the time to prayer. We all sat cross-legged in an awkward circle on the old carpeted floor. As the phrase echoed in my head, our teacher taught us the heart prayer, "Lord Jesus Christ, Son of God, have mercy on me a sinner." A prayer by St. Paul is, "pray without ceasing." It gave a name to the phenomenon that was going on inside my head. God had a reason for me to attend that class.

The *heart prayer* silently repeated itself the entire drive to the hospital with my uncle. The closer we got to the hospital the stronger the prayer was in my head. It pounded while I rushed through those hospital halls, the path already imprinted on my mind from previous visits.

It stopped the moment I entered Grandpa's room. My family sat squished around his bedside. I walked to the end of his bed. My emotions blended sadness, dread, and hope. All that praying, just so I was allowed this moment. But I wasn't ready for this goodbye. Grandpa Bud's eyes fluttered open. "Hi, Princess," he said.

My *heart prayer* produced a small miracle. Grandpa Bud lived for many months after that. One day, I prayed, "He's ready to go, and I'm ready for the Holy Spirit to take him." That was my goodbye.

I have no doubt that Grandpa visited me in that dream two years later. I felt God's Spirit through these experiences. The Spirit whispered to me that I possess both the power of prayer and the strength to believe in heaven. So, it is with a full heart that I say, "Thank you, Holy Spirit, and Grandpa Bud. I hope this story makes you smile."

The Spirit Whispered: You know the power of prayer and your faith is strong. I know you are grateful. I watched how you loved your grandpa. Don't worry, he is happy and at peace.

Prayer: Divine Spirit, I am thankful to you for all that you have done for me. For the times when my faith wavered, I hope you'll forgive me. And if ever I should despair, remind me of the power of prayer.

Katie Saunders, *Neuroscience*
Pittsford, MI

"Dear God, I need you to fill me
with excitement once again.
Please awaken my Spirit.
I feel like I have been out of focus
and asleep for so long.
Lord wake me up and return me
to the land of the living."

Karen Kostyla

Whisper Twenty-Four: God's Mission

Five years ago, I signed up to go on a mission trip to Georgia. I was a junior in High School at the time, and very involved in my church youth group. I had many friends who had also decided to participate in the week of service. Despite the scorching heat and the difficult manual labor ahead of us, we knew that God would be faithful, and our experience would be one of a lifetime.

From our hometown of Grand Haven, Michigan to Milan, Georgia, it was supposed to take 14 and a half hours. Two hours and 45 minutes into the trip, we stopped at McDonald's for breakfast in Dundee, Michigan. When we pulled into the McDonald's parking lot, the driver of the 12-passenger van noticed that the "check engine" light was on. Knowing we still had a long journey ahead of us, he decided to take the van to the nearest shop while we ate our breakfast. About two hours later, he returned with a disgruntled face. We received news that the van blew a spark plug, and would need to be in the shop for another hour to be fixed. Because the McDonald's crew was getting fed up by our large, and zealous crowd, we decided to take the other two vans across the street to Cabela's where we could hangout while the van got fixed. After trying every hammock, and checking out every piece of hunting gear that you could imagine, we finally got the van back and hit the road.

At this point, everyone was feeling relieved that we could continue our journey. We were a few hours behind schedule, but with our mission in mind, we headed onward. If you've ever taken the trip from Western Michigan, to Georgia, you know it's not the most exciting drive. As we drove through hours of flat, empty land in Ohio, we had to get creative with our travel entertainment. Luckily, with 20 high school students, it's never boring. Once we finally made it to Kentucky, I started seeing beautiful green mountains up ahead. The scenery was breathtaking, and the sky was bright blue so we decided to stop in the Appalachians for a picnic. As I was sitting on a warm rock, eating my peanut butter sandwich, everything seemed perfect. Our trip was going smoothly, we were making good headway, and we were able to enjoy a gorgeous mountaintop view. However, God still had more planned for us.

As we got back in the vans and continued to wind through the mountains, the "check engine" light in the van appeared again. Upon hearing this news, I remember thinking "Really?! Are we ever going to get to Georgia?! Why does this keep happening? We are trying to do God's work!" It didn't make sense to me. We pulled into the parking lot of a gas station, which seemed to be in the middle of nowhere. The local Kentucky people pulled up to get their fill of gas and snacks as we sat in the van listening to the chaperones try to figure out what to do.

Our Youth Minister, Chris, went inside to ask the employees if there was a nearby hotel that we could all stay for the night. Sadly, because we were in the middle of nowhere, there was not. When he returned to the group, a man walked up to him and asked where we were headed. Even though Chris had no desire for small talk, he kindly replied that we were all headed down to Georgia for a week of mission work. The man responded with an enthusiastic statement of approval. He congratulated us for taking the time out of our busy schedules to help the poor, and to make the long drive to get down there. Then, he asked Chris if he could pray with all of us, that we would make it to our destination if that was in God's will. We all gathered around the man as he prayed over us.

After the prayer, God presented us with an opportunity that none of us could have imagined. The man looked at us, and turned toward Chris. He said, "Chris, y'all seem like such a wonderful group. I don't know of a hotel that you can stay at, but, I run a mission just up the road called God's Closet. We are a non-profit organization that collects new and gently worn clothing for families in need. We run a free shop-day for families, where we only charge a $1.00 entrance fee. We have about 15 bunk beds. Nobody is staying with us this week, and we could really use the help for our free-shop day. I would love for y'all to stay with us a day or two and help out while your van gets fixed." We were all amazed! If running into a guy that runs a mission and needs help while we're on a MISSION TRIP isn't a "God wink," then I don't know what is! Our drivers were tired, and there was no way we were getting out of that town (which by the way is called London, Kentucky) that night, so we took the man up on his offer and drove a few miles up the mountain until we saw a medium-sized, white building, with large letters spelling out, "God's Closet" above the front door.

We spent the next three days working in the Kentucky heat, organizing racks of clothing, painting the walls, and spreading God's love through a praise and worship session. The people who visited the mission were thankful for the young, friendly faces, and the new, free clothes. I felt God's presence in the work that we accomplished, and the people we met. It was amazing to witness the store in action because it was built on such a wonderful foundation.

After three days we took the vans down to Georgia where we were supposed to have been serving from the beginning. The funny thing to me was that when we arrived, there wasn't as much work to be done as we had originally planned. We split up into small work groups to fix porches and stairs, clean up church property, and to paint the inside of the church's welcome center. By the end of our trip, we were able to complete all of the work that we had originally planned on finishing during the full week.

When I look back on this trip, one of my favorite scripture verses comes to mind. Proverbs 3:5: "Trust in the Lord with all your heart, and lean not on your own understanding; in all your ways acknowledge him, and he shall direct your paths."

Although we had planned our entire itinerary for the mission trip, we had let go of our plan. When things started to go wrong we had to put our complete trust in God. When we surrendered to his itinerary, he led us down a completely different path than the one we had intended. Because of this, we were able to serve people we had no idea needed our help. In what we thought was an inconvenience, God reminded us who we really were serving. I can't imagine what would have happened if we hadn't stopped for gas in that little town, and I can't fathom what frustration we would have felt if we hadn't decided to invite the Holy Spirit to be our trip navigator. We couldn't see the big picture, but God could, and our reward for listening to his call and trusting him when we couldn't see that picture was far more incredible and memorable than we could have ever imagined.

The Spirit Whispered: Live every day according to God's plan, and not your own. Trust the Spirit to guide you down his virtuous pathway. Invite the Lord to be your navigator each day. You are the driver and you get to choose the ultimate direction in which you travel, but when you take the road of virtue he has paved for you, your final destination will take your breath away. When your plans are elaborate, know that even then, his plans are far more extravagant.

Prayer: Divine Spirit, help us to trust you in times of darkness or confusion. We look up to you so that you may make our paths straight. Our hands and hearts are yours to use for serving those who need them.

Claire Miles, *Elementary Education*
Grand Haven, MI

Whisper Twenty-Five: God's Love is Massive

My first experience of Christ was during the summer before my freshman year of high school. As I was kneeling in adoration at a Steubenville Youth Conference, the priest leading the time of prayer said: "Don't overcomplicate your prayer. Simply ask the Lord *one* question you have. My question was "Lord, do you love me, and if so, how much?" It was a simple question, and I got a simple answer. Not a voice from the sky or anything like that, but a simple response in my heart. "Yes, more than you will *ever* know." This first true experience of God's love forever molded my heart. My faith since then has been built on this love.

During the summer of 2014, I went on an eight day Ignatian silent retreat. During the retreat, I had daily "themes" to meditate on using scripture. The retreat was an amazing experience of looking through my life, seeking healing from Christ in areas of hurt, and thanking him for areas of success. In my daily scripture meditations, I truly discovered Christ. I learned how much he loves me once again. This wasn't an intellectual learning, simply a rediscovery, a deepening of my whole being accepting Christ's love more fully.

During day four of the retreat, I had a bit of a breakdown. I didn't realize how much I use the things of each day to hide from myself and from God. I had even used prayer as a way to hide from facing myself and God, and seeking and receiving his healing. But after facing God for four straight days in silence with no personal contact with anyone but my spiritual director, I lost it. I had heard about this type of experience from others who had done silent retreats, but now it was happening to me. God needed me to completely break down, so he could pick up the pieces and reshape me in a better way. Needless to say, that fourth day was tough, and I even was tempted to leave the retreat. But God's grace mysteriously pulled me through.

As I lay in bed at the end of the fourth day, I tossed and turned, still shaken up by the breakdown and the rebuilding I was facing. At about 11:30, after two hours of restless sleep, I heard a voice, a voice I had come to very clearly and easily hear during this retreat.
It was Jesus, and who simply said, "Come to me."

71

I wasn't happy. "Jesus, seriously, it is 11:30 and I just want some sleep. I was in that chapel for five hours today. Isn't that enough?"

I resisted for about 10 minutes, but finally, I gave in to him. "Fine, I'm coming. See, I'm walking. Here I come."

I slowly walked into the chapel, and walked to the tabernacle. I rested my head on it, sighed, and said, "Alright Jesus, what do you want."

He quietly replied, "Oh, I forgot to say goodnight to you."

What? You forgot to say goodnight?

Here is the God of the Universe, who created everything, who died for me, and he forgot to say goodnight. I could almost picture him in there, just thinking "What excuse can I have to see him for one more second. What can I... then, I got it! I'll ask him to come so I can say goodnight."

What God would do to have me for one more second in his presence? I was so focused on the big picture and receiving God's love in big ways. It wasn't as if these big things were unimportant. But in this moment, in this short two minute encounter with Jesus Christ, I learned more about Jesus's love than from all of my previous "knowledge" combined. I experienced the intimate, all-caring love that Jesus Christ has for us all. It was simply about one more second with me, one more second spent with him, for which he would do anything; even die on the cross again.

The Spirit Whispered: Come to me. I love you more than you will ever know. I would do anything for even ONE MORE SECOND with you. I would even die on the cross for you, just for that one second.

Prayer: Divine Spirit, give me the grace to receive your love as completely and fully as I can. Allow me to experience your love more and more each day. Grant that today, the conversion I have this morning will forever change me.

Joshua Hamilton, *Co-Director of "The Catholic Media Project"*
Fowler, MI

"Today I will ask myself
what I really want
and listen to the
whispers of my soul."

The Gossamer Path

Whisper Twenty-Six: Whisper from the Heart: The Lion King

I know God loves us because God speaks to us. When we get mad at someone, what's the first thing we do? We stop talking to that person. Well God never stops speaking to us. God gave me one message. When Jesus was born, God wanted to give the good news to the people of Belen, so he sent them an angel. He spoke to them through an angel. To the wise kings on the other hand, he gave them the same message but through a star. God didn't say "An angel for all, if you understood great, and if you don't, then too bad." God speaks in many ways. God knows people learn in different ways. I am a very big fan of Disney Movies. The message whispered to me was through the form of a Disney Movie.

Since my time at Michigan State, I have seen people change. I have seen people lose themselves to the ways of the world. While praying for teens here and all over the world, God revealed to me an analogy. I'm sure we have all seen The Lion King, at least once, a very old Disney film. In the Lion King, there is a small lion who, because of his Uncle Scar, has to leave his lands and run away to the deserted lands. Simba comes across Timon and Pumba. Simba is scared, nervous, and afraid. Timon and Pumba find Simba in the middle of nowhere. They see him worried and panicked and say *"Hakuna Matata.* It means no worries for the rest of your days. It's our problem-free philosophy, Hakuna Matata." Hakuna Matata means don't worry be happy, relax. Timon and Pumba feed Simba bugs, and change the way he used to live. Simba starts doing things he didn't do before he met them. Simba starts eating bugs, he changes his diet because of friends. He grows up doing these things. Like Simba, we come to college afraid of what might be, we find friends who are Timon and Pumba's who try to change us too, make us eat different, act different, speak different, etc.

Nala, who was Simba's best friend when they were young, comes up in the middle of the movie, she recognizes Simba and tells him "Simba I thought you were dead!" Simba is more alive than ever, he's all about Hakuna Matata and living a stress free lifestyle. Simba even tries to convince Nala to stay there and change her lifestyle too. Nala, though, does not let him. She reminds him that his place is back home in the kingdom. He has abandoned his spot as king and that's why things back home are bad. Simba denies it and his friends Timon and Pumba laugh at him saying, "King? What King! He's no King!" Nala firmly says, "You are King. You are the heir of the throne. Things are bad because you have abandoned your responsibilities." Like Simba, we too because of the ways of the world can abandon our faith and our values here in college. And like Simba, when we keep steady in our faith, our friends Timon and Pumba might laugh and say, "Church? Why church?"

Simba goes to a small river to drink water and in the water he sees his Father Mufasa's reflection. His father reminds him, "Remember who you are!" In that moment Simba realizes he is king and he runs back home to claim his spot as king. We too need to remember who we are. And I myself, being a college student, can forget at times who I am and what I stand for.

We teens are Simba. We let our sins scare us away from God. Especially here in college, we meet people who are Timons and Pumbas. People who try to tell us: Don't worry about church. Go have fun! Smoke, drink, have sex, consume it all! Why study so much? Why pray? Why sacrifice so much? Why work so hard? Go out and live life. You only live once, HAKUNA MATATA!!!

We are all a Prince or Princess, because like Simba we are the sons and daughters of a King much bigger than Mufasa! We are the sons and daughters of the King of Kings. We are the sons and daughters of God! We are the future of the church, the future of the world. When Simba got back to his kingdom, things were bad, things were wrong. But he got there and things started changing for the better. With us too, what world are we living in? What are we doing to change the world? Are we just sitting around saying Hakuna Matata? Are we going to stay with our friends Timon and Pumba, or are we going to take up our responsibilities in the world, in the church.

Friends like Timon and Pumba lead to a mediocre lifestyle. "Let's pray a little, let's work a little, just enough to get by, don't take life too seriously." Only we can make the choice. No matter how many friends we have who are like Nala who try to remind us where we truly belong. It is ultimately up to us to make the choice. God tells us, "Remember who you are."

The Spirit Whispered: Listen to me. I am always here for you.

Prayer: Divine Spirit, speak to us in ways, so we can understand you and do your will. Divine Spirit, give us friends, to remind us to return to you in times of temptation. Care for us, when surrounded by those who tempt us.

Selena Huapilla-Perez, *Elementary Education*
East Lansing, MI

"As we dwell in solitude and
cultivate interior silence,
we learn to listen for the
consoling whispers of God."

John Dear

Whisper Twenty-Seven: The Small Things in Life

Sometimes I feel like I convince myself that a lot of the things I struggle with on a daily basis are so inconsequential to my life that it means it would be wrong of me to pray or ask God for help with the difficulty. However, in the course of keeping my problems humble, it also creates the illusion that I don't need God's help with the smaller things in my life, or to an extent that I can handle it on my own, or that maybe he doesn't even care.

A situation arose when I had to decide what to do for a lab I took with my Technical Theater class. This lab required everyone to help with the backstage crew for one of the Theater Department's fall productions. I was trying to decide between the last two, but neither one seemed to be ideal as both of them would cause me to miss out on things I really wanted to go to, such as a family tailgate, a rivalry football game, or the fall retreat at my church. I knew it wasn't really that big of a deal and I would just have to make some sacrifices, but the decision kept nagging at me and very quickly it began to overpower my life. I constantly worried about it and debated back and forth, writing pro and con lists and all sorts of things that just kept me spinning in circles.

Finally, I made the decision to ask God for help. I approached it by basically saying, "Jesus, I know this decision isn't even close to life or death, but it is really bothering me, so I could use a little help. Please somehow show me which decision you want me to make because I know I will be happier with whatever you think best." I asked that he give me some sort of sign that I would recognize as him within three days, and then kicked back, waiting for the answer to fall onto my lap on a silver platter.

The next three days were the most stressful I ever had during this decision-making process. I kept frantically going back and forth worried that I wouldn't get the sign, then assuring myself I would, and then back again. As the days slowly crept by, nothing seemed to be showing up and I was to the point that I would start over-analyzing everything people said to me, trying to find something that would give me the answer. But nothing did.

It was 11:00 pm on the third day and I was just about to lose hope, thinking things such as "I must've done something wrong," or, "It doesn't even matter that much, so why should God be bothered just by this stupid thing?" I grudgingly went to bed, opened my Jesus Calling book by Sarah Young and there, on the reflection for September 17, was my answer.

"You will not find my peace by engaging in excessive planning, attempting to control what happens to you in the future. When your mind spins with multiple plans, peace may sometimes seem to be within your grasp; yet it always eludes you. Commit everything into my care. Turn from the path of planning to the path of peace," and at once I felt complete peace for the first time during this entire process.

It wasn't at all the answer I expected, and most people would look at this and say it wasn't even an answer, but I instantly knew in my heart that this was God telling me he heard my prayer and cares about what I'm doing, no matter how big or small. He used this three day period of waiting, not to torment me, but to teach me that worrying and trying to control everything will not help, but instead I need to learn to give him control and trust where he will take me.

Now I will be the first to admit that this is much easier said than done, but God whispered to my heart exactly what I needed to hear. Incidentally, about five minutes after I read that reflection, I talked the decision over with my mom and the decision suddenly became so obvious that I had no idea how I hadn't seen it before. God does work in ways that we don't expect, and even don't like at the time. Looking back on it, I wouldn't change a thing because I learned an important lesson and got to experience having a personal encounter with the Lord. I asked and was given, and God loves me enough to help me with all my cares, big or small, as he does for every single person.

The Spirit Whispered: I want you to commit everything into my care. I will give you a peace your heart so longs for, just trust in me.

Prayer: Divine Spirit, grant me the ability to search for God in all that I do, and to always be open to hearing his word and doing his will. Give me patience and peace in all decisions I make, large or small, and help me to always include you in everything I do.

Kristin Collins, *Interior Design*
Grand Rapids, MI

"'Trust me.'
The words came as a
gentle whisper
to her soul…"

Author Unknown

Whisper Twenty-Eight: A Fire in the Dead of Night

I walked into the chapel for adoration of the Eucharist at 2:02 am. Kneeling, I placed my headphones over my ears and played Deus Est Lux II, an ethereal prayer-focused music mix by Graphite412. After about 10 minutes or so of struggling to feel God's presence, I asked God to show me a sign that he was listening. I prayed with open arms so as to show God that I wanted to let him into my heart. Several minutes later, a girl wrapped in a light blue blanket walked in, paused in front of the altar, and went onto her hands and knees.

At that point, I knew that God had answered my prayer and I burst into a smile. The fact that God had given a gentle push to someone at 2:15 am to go and pray in the chapel as soon as I asked him is beyond words. I praised his name and gave thanks for all that God had blessed me with in my life. Then after about five minutes, I noticed that another person also came in for adoration. Thanking the Lord yet again for reaffirming my prayer, I felt that I was washed over with a wave of peace. As soon as my music mix ended, I went and prostrated myself in the middle aisle, just in front of the altar.

Throughout my meditation, I asked Jesus, "Why would you take up my sin onto that cross and die for my sake?"

I replayed images of Jesus getting nailed to the cross over and over again in my head. Suddenly, I realized that my image of Jesus was always looking toward the sky, or rather, heaven. I heard a whisper, "I died for you so you can live. And to live is to love, and to love is to be a disciple of Jesus Christ." Jesus wanted me to be a man of God just as he was on earth. After my revelation, I looked at the monstrance and got a sense of something telling me, "Now go, get up and follow me." I got up and slowly departed not forgetting what I heard in that whisper.

The Spirit Whispered: I died so that you could live, and to truly live is to love. To be a true disciple of Jesus Christ you have to be a reflection of me. I want you to be a man of God and follow in my footsteps, as you spread the message of love and forgiveness.

Prayer: Divine Spirit, you set fire to each and every heart with zeal for a closer relationship with our loving father. Thank you for enkindling me so that my fire can warm those who have hearts of ice. With your help, draw me closer to your ever-burning love.

Mateusz Marek Spiewla, *Computer Science*
East Lansing, MI

Whisper Twenty-Nine: Healing a Hardened Heart

The Spirit has always been working in my life and God has always held my hand through the hardships. However, I can think of one specific experience in which I began to really feel the Spirit. After years of friendship, two people that I had really loved for years hurt me. I was unable to wrap my head around their actions and I took it as personally as could be. For so long, the incident gave me so much bitterness and anger. I had never felt so betrayed in my life. I asked God why this was happening. I asked him what he was going to do to make it right. I was so concerned about the actions of others that I had completely disregarded my own. I had begun to let my negative experience become a part of me. During this time, I thankfully stumbled upon this quote:

"Throughout life people will make you mad, disrespect you, and treat you bad. Let God deal with the things they do, cause the hate in your heart will consume you too." -Will Smith.

Seeing this quote really affected me. I began to pray on the matter and ask God for guidance. It wasn't very long after that I realized what I needed was healing. Hatred had hardened my heart and consumed me. Coming upon this realization, I knew I had to change my thinking. I began to accept that God took those people out of my life for better ones to be placed in it. Through prayer, I let the Holy Spirit heal my heart. I knew I had to forgive them in order for me to begin healing. I read this passage several times:

"Get rid of all bitterness, rage and anger, brawling and slander, along with every form of malice. Be kind and compassionate to one another, forgiving each other, just as in Christ God forgave you." -Ephesians 4:31-32

The most difficult part of forgiving was that they weren't even asking me for forgiveness. Once again, the Spirit whispered love and healing into my heart. I let go of the bitterness, rage, and anger, I stopped gossiping about how others have wronged me, and I slowly began to forgive. As time moved on, I established new relationships in my life, became happier, and let go of the past. God removed the toxic from my life and heart to make room for better things.

The Spirit Whispered: Forgive others for what they have done to you, for hatred will harden your heart and consume you.

Prayer: Divine Spirit, remind me to let go of the grudges I may hold over someone. Please remind me that you have a plan for my life and that the people you have come and go in it are there for a reason. Through your name I pray.

Kristen Dantonio, *Elementary Education*
East Lansing, MI

Whisper Thirty: Spiritual Nourishment

The minute I heard about Sister Dorothy's book, I knew I wanted to contribute. The only question was, "What will my story be?" I had felt the Spirit working in my life many times, but which story to choose?

Well, it was a busy time in the fall semester of my senior year and, consequently, I hadn't had time to think about writing other than when it surfaced from my subconscious and knocked around my harried head, reminding me of how I needed to make time to pray about my story.

Then finally the day arrived, a Tuesday night free of obligations. Where better than to write about my encounter with the Spirit than the place where I feel closest to God, where I am truly in the presence of Jesus, at Eucharistic Adoration.

Walking into St. John's my mind hummed with ideas... none of which related to my story. I was pondering Honors projects, exams, and general end-of-the-semester business. I was also trying to determine what to say to a close friend who had texted me about her frustrations with her roommate.

My mind felt heavy with these thick thoughts as I pulled a quote out of the "Spiritual Nourishment" jar that Sr. Dorothy has placed by the sink after washing my hands. It was as if the little crimson card already knew my heart and how overwhelmed I was, unsure of where to turn or what to do. It so simply and beautifully read "If you can't find the right words to use, use the words you have. If you're not sure what to do, just get busy and do what you can."

After reading it, a smile spread across my face. I felt the quiet peace of the Holy Spirit. I knew the Spirit would give me the words I needed to help my friend and the energy to accomplish all I needed to in order to finish the semester strong. The heavy thoughts floated away. Just one remained: that moment and the sense of peace I felt after reading the quote was the perfect story to contribute to the book. The Spirit had whispered to me through the "Spiritual Nourishment" quote at the time I needed it most.

For me this story shows how the Holy Spirit always watches over us and helps us along the way as we confront life's struggles. Whether it be finding the right words, tackling seemingly insurmountable tasks, or simply walking along the path God has provided for us, the Spirit is always there to guide us through the journey.

The Spirit Whispered: I am always with you. Even when you are distracted and disconnected, I am always working in your life. Look for me in all things.

Prayer: Divine Spirit, walk beside me on this journey God has set before me. Watch over me and help me during times of need and times of abundance. Help me know that I am not alone, for you are always with me. Divine Spirit, walk beside me.

Molly Robbins, *Kinesiology*
Washington, MI

Whisper Thirty-One: Now I Hear You

Communication is the most important thing in a relationship. When I was four years old, I told my neighbor, "If we want to be friends, we have to communicate." Verbal communication has always been a strong suit of mine allowing me to make strong connections with the people I meet.

After attending Academy of the Sacred Heart of Bloomfield Hills for high school, I had a very strong foundation for my academics and my relationship with God. I had a clear-cut image of what I expected college to be like – perfect grades, immediate friends, and minimal homesickness. Sadly that was not the case. After my first month, in college life I struggled on my first few exams, struggled to meet people who were like me, and considered switching universities.

The Nebraska versus Michigan State football game came around in the beginning of October and I was not a hundred percent sure where I was emotionally. I sat with my dad and close family friends of ours whom we have known for years. Two of my mom's sorority sisters realized something was wrong and I broke down. I admitted that I was not sure what I was doing and was not sure I made the right decision coming to such a large school. One of my mom's friends randomly stopped the conversation telling me she knew a nun that would be able to introduce me to a wonderful community. She texted Sister Dorothy telling her she had a girl who needed a community to be a part of. I was rushed to this football suite where Sister Dorothy was with her sister. My mom's friend introduced me to Sister Dorothy. We chatted and she invited me to sign up for a fall retreat. I was excited and could not wait to get back to the parish and sign up for the retreat.

About three months after I met Sister Dorothy, she introduced me to two of my best friends. These two friends have been people I can trust with my life and listen to me when I am having a rough time. As for hearing God, that took until Ash Wednesday of this current Lenten season. I had met with the head of my high school that past Monday, I left with not knowing how to respond to the advice she had given me. She told me to sit quietly, clear your mind, and listen.

This was a struggle for me because my mind is very unquiet, therefore, getting it to calm can be very difficult.

Sitting in church, once receiving ashes and Holy Communion, I sat in my pew singing Amazing Grace; I prayed for a clear mind, a clear look at the path I was on, and where I was supposed to go with my life. I needed to see where I was going with my life after some bad news I received that prior weekend. My mind suddenly was clear, calm and serene, like never before. I did not hear a voice but I had a much better understanding of where my life was going. Having this moment changed how I looked at prayer and how I interpreted what God is saying to me on a daily basis. My mind is now clear and I have overcame prior struggles that I never thought I would. Starting with complete silence to now being able to communicate with the Lord is an incredible thing. I have been able to put full trust in God and I now have full confidence in my future.

The Spirit Whispered: Be still. Clear your mind of all anxiety and fear I will take care of you and guide you.

Prayer: Divine Spirit, please grant me the virtue of patience that I will be able to discover God's path for me.

Charlotte Stechschulte, *Pre-Nursing*
Rochester, MI

Whisper Thirty-Two: A Moment of Vulnerability

Throughout high school, I lived the typical Catholic student lifestyle: go to Mass, go to confession, and parrot back answers to teachers in school. At that point, I didn't realize that I was living in a bubble of sorts, wearing a face of complacency while just running through the motions. So when I went to college at Michigan State, the challenge was going to be how I would strengthen my faith life without the guidance of parents and teachers that I had access to back home. I did the same thing I did in high school, simply going to Mass on Sundays, until my class schedule and extra-curricular activities began to take over my life. At that point, I stopped going to Mass and I only focused on schoolwork. I felt this emptiness inside that following summer when I realized how far away from God I felt. That next year, I decided I would make a more concerted effort to get involved at St. John's. I went on the fall retreat, volunteered to go on an Alternative Spring Break trip to Jonestown, and ended up leading the spring retreat. I started going to Mass on Tuesday and Thursday nights, which brought me a sense of peace and connection with the Holy Spirit. That year, I became one with the community of students. Their faith and love for God really inspired me to be better in my faith life, and I strived to do more to strengthen my relationship with God.

The following year, my junior year, my goal was to refuse to get into a rut again. Sophomore year was so dynamic for me, so there was always the worry I would have a letdown of sorts or just become satisfied with how far I had come in my journey. But having a relationship with God is so much more than that. It is an ongoing process, a path of continual improvement. I led the fall retreat that year and signed up for another Alternative Spring Break trip to the same location as the previous year. After leading a retreat twice in a row, I went on the spring retreat as a participant, which involves a much different mindset. I made what I believe to be one of the biggest steps in my faith journey that weekend, when I had the best confession of my life. I was inspired by the talk of a fellow student and opened up to the priest in a way that I had never done before. I cut out all the "fluff" that many confessions contain, being unspecific, and scared of what the priest would think. But I opened up. I let the doctor see my wound, so he could heal it. And I was transformed. At

91

adoration immediately after, I was moved to tears when I was in the presence of Christ, and I knew I would never be the same again. God was in my life, and I was never going to let go again.

The Spirit Whispered: Do not be afraid to be vulnerable, that I might heal all your wounds. Open yourself to healing and forgiveness, and you will be one with me.

Prayer: Divine Spirit, thank you for your limitless desire for me to be one with you, despite all my shortcomings, flaws, and weakness. Help those who are looking for the strength to become closer with you. Amen

Anthony Garvert, *Electrical Engineering*
Naperville, IL

Whisper Thirty-Three: You are Never Alone – Just Trust

When Jesus calls us to be strong, part of this call is to remain faithful to his plan even when we hit bumps in the road. It is not easy to remain calm and pursue an attitude of trust when we are in a crisis, and I certainly understand that. In March 2012, I had an emergency appendectomy over spring break. Initially, I was not too worried since I remember my dad going through the same thing a few years before, but unfortunately, I faced several complications from the surgery and the road to recovery was much longer than anticipated. I was devastated about having to leave MSU for the semester. How was I going to survive without my closest friends by my side? Would people forget about me? When I initially had thoughts like this, I took my anger out on God. How was I supposed to find the positive aspects of this situation?

Then, one day, I pulled out my phone and mass texted many close friends at Michigan State University. I knew I had to let them know the situation I was in, and I asked for prayers for strength and perseverance. Within an hour, I received countless messages in return that reassured me I was not alone on my journey to recovery. My friends reached out to me in so many ways, whether it was saying a rosary for me, offering to come visit me in the hospital, or calling me on the phone when I needed to talk. I then realized I was silly to ever think I was alone. Jesus never lets us walk alone, even in the darkest of times.

The Spirit Whispered: You are never alone – just trust in me.

Prayer: Divine Spirit, Father, fill our hearts with deep compassion for those who suffer, and may the day come quickly of your kingdom of justice and truth.

Paula Bobosky, *Human Development and Family Studies*
Farmington Hills, MI

"Each whisper from your heart
is a potential boarding pass
for the next leg of your journey
that is your life.
Where will you fly to next?"

Author Unknown

Whisper Thirty-Four: The Difference Between a "Problem and an Inconvenience"

It was the day after my 18th birthday, I was watching rehearsals of my high school's production of, "All I Really Need to Know I Learned in Kindergarten." I was not in a good mood because the night before, I had a conversation with a friend of mine who I had feelings for, and questions of mine weren't answered. The cast was acting out Ed's scene where he recalls a memory about venting to Sigmund Wollman, an Auschwitz survivor, about eating the same meal every day. When Ed is done ranting, Sigmund says:

"You don't know the difference between a problem and an inconvenience."

That line resounded throughout my mind. I said to myself, "The difference between a problem and an inconvenience? How does that apply to my situation?"

I met my friend during my freshman year of high school. Since we had similar interests and personalities, we cultivated an amazing friendship. She was a caring, genuine, and trustworthy individual I could talk to about anything. Through our conversations, we learned of each other's problems with people we liked, and hoped for the best for each other. Now, while my issue was resolved, her problem was not.

My junior year of high school, I acquired two tickets to an orchestra concert, and knowing that she loves those kinds of music, I figured she would be interested in going. I asked her, and she happily agreed. I picked her up, and we had a wonderful time. At the end of the evening we had an interesting conversation, in which I promised her I would write her a song which would be the most beautiful song she would ever hear. She responded, "Looking forward to hearing it. Who knows? Maybe someday you and I will be together. You never know what time will bring."

What?

I hadn't expected this response. Even though she had said this twice, it took me by surprise, while setting off some butterflies in my stomach. I respond, saying, "Maybe, I will think about it."

The next day, I woke up with a lump in my throat, and those butterflies still fluttering around. Thinking about that conversation, I wondered whether I should ask her what she meant by that statement. No matter what I did, I couldn't stop thinking about the conversation. It bugged me the whole day, and those butterflies wouldn't stop fluttering. Was this me developing feelings for this girl? It was.

Before I could ask her about it, she brought up her boyfriend, the person from my freshman year whom she had feelings for since sixth grade, for seven years.

I finally got up enough nerve and asked her what she meant that night. Her response, "I don't think it would be good for us to get into a relationship now because I'm headed off to college, and I still have unresolved issues with Alex."

I understood her side of it. It seemed to me if this guy, who is in college in Oregon, hadn't returned feelings for her by now, he's not going to anytime soon. So move on. Obviously, this is easier said than done. I didn't give her the advice because I didn't want to hurt her feelings. We didn't communicate for several weeks.

Weeks went by and I was at summer camp at Interlochen. I texted her and we had short, but nice conversations. A few days later, I received a text from her saying, "Wish I could text you right now. Miss you!" The butterflies came again. I was confused as to whether she had feelings for me or not?

Meanwhile, we wrote letters to each other, and she came to attend the last composer's concert of the camp. When I saw she was there, I was elated. But, much to my dismay, the time flew and she had to leave.

Later, I received a text from her, and our conversation leads to us talking about our futures. I talked about us being a famous musical duo, and she said, "I'll just be the amazing wife supporting you."

Whoa...

Wife? First you're thinking of a relationship, and now my wife? It's such a strong word. I was elated. I responded in a way to which she later said, "We will be together forever."

After a few conversations I asked her out, it was our first date. However, it didn't go well. After a few days, I asked her out again, and she agreed, but said, "We'll figure it out." This same thing happened for a few more weeks, so I gave up for a while.

On my birthday, I was having a good day, and while talking with her, she mentioned a book she was reading. It was frustrating her because the two main characters have a romantic connection with each other, but neither of them would do anything about it.

Sound familiar?

I asked her if she saw us in that book, to which she said, "I don't know, maybe." She was concerned about how college will change everything. I said that I didn't want this to be a hardship on her, and we didn't need to make this difficult. If we wanted to get to know each other better, then we're the biggest obstacle. She said it wasn't a hardship, and that it's only her getting in the way.

At least she recognized what I knew all along: her indecisiveness was preventing us from being together. I said, "We had nothing to be nervous about because were too young," She agreed. I said, "I hope we could have some fun soon." Her response, "We'll figure it out."

At that point, whenever I read that, the hurt feelings resurfaced, it finally occurred to me that she'd never been in a real relationship. When I thought of this, everything clicked because it made perfect sense as to why she was acting this way.

The problem was her indecisiveness. The inconvenience was college. Was it inconvenient that she was hardly available because of her schedule? Yes, but I understood it. Was I willing to put up with the inconvenience in order to be with someone who might be "the one," or should I give up because of the problem? After she said that it would be easier to do this when we're both in college, I had to agree.

Later that week, we talked again, and I said that if we were to get involved, she had nothing to worry about on my part because I wouldn't hurt her. After responding with "What if you left?" I responded by saying that I loved her, and that I wouldn't hurt her. After she responded with "That is the nicest thing anyone has ever said to me." We exchanged a few words, and didn't talk for days.

Eventually, we went on that second date, which went well. But, when we said goodbye, she told me, "I don't think we are a good fit for a relationship."

It hit me like a brick wall. I went into deep depression. I tried to explain a few times how I felt, but her responses seemed like she could care less, which only magnified my pain.

It was the night before my first college class. I was talking with her, and out of nowhere, she said, "I'm in a new relationship, and I wanted to tell you before you found out from somebody else."

Now, in 2015, we still talk occasionally, but it's not the same. I've grown much stronger in my faith than I was then, and after much reflection and praying, I've learned two things: don't waste your time pining for someone, and put your trust in God about everything, even relationships. God understands and is always there for you. God won't lead you astray.

Do you think I absolutely regret not praying about this "relationship," and putting God at the center of it? Absolutely! Had I done that, maybe things would've been different. If God wants it to happen, it will happen. Give everything to God and his abundant grace will be poured upon you.

The Spirit Whispered: Learn to trust in me. I am with you always, in the good times and bad. Seek me, and everything will fall into place.

Prayer: Divine Spirit, help me to trust in you more. Help me to be more attentive to your will, and to be humble enough to listen and live out that will.

Michael Garnett, *Conductor/Composer/Music Minister*
East Lansing, MI

"Prayer,
meaningful prayer can
always be a part of your life."

Fr. Jim Lothamer

Whisper Thirty-Five: The Silent Sheep

Coming to St. John's has been the most motivational way to increase my relationship with God at Michigan State University [MSU.] Growing up in a Catholic family, I understood what it meant to be a Catholic but there were ways that I grew in faith that I never would have accomplished at home. There is such a wide variety of activities to join such as men's group, campus bible study, and priesthood discernment group that have helped me grow spiritually and socially throughout my time at MSU.

Throughout high school, I was always a decently faithful Christian, but I was nowhere as close to God as I became throughout my time at St. John's. My biggest struggle in spirituality was consistency. As I became more involved at St. John's, I felt more of a desire to encounter God in a more intimate way. I learned to start praying the rosary and reading scripture at least three times a week, go to daily Mass, adoration, and confession at least once or twice a week, and became a part of an awesome community.

My favorite form of prayer, besides Mass of course, is sitting in silence in front of the Blessed Sacrament. Giving the opportunity for God to communicate to me instead of always talking to him is a way of growing in spirituality that I can only achieve through silence. I always listen for answers to questions of what possible vocations I might be called to and any general questions that I am anxious about for my future. Time after time of sitting in silence, I am beginning to understand God's whisper to me. God does not want me to be stressed about my future or what my vocation is. The Spirit whispers to me, "Focus on me and you will find happiness."

There are many times in my life where I lose my focus on God and just when I do not know what to do, he tells me to focus on him. Knowing that I have a God who has the perfect plan in the world for me gives me an unexplainable comforting sensation. I have only one part to play: focus on Jesus. Just like the lost sheep that went astray in the gospel because it lost its focus on Jesus, I feel like that lost sheep when I lose my focus on God. So the Spirit whispers to me

"Focus on me," and those words take me back on the path to his kingdom.

The Spirit Whispered: Focus on me and you will find happiness and fulfillment.

Prayer: Divine Spirit, help me to focus my love on you. Grant me the faith that I may not stray from your mercy and compassion. Teach me to be your faithful servant.

Francis Dallo, *Professional Writing*
Southfield, MI

Whisper Thirty-Six: My Call Back to God

During spring break of my freshman year of high school, my parents received a call from my family in Lebanon informing them that my mom's mother hadn't been feeling well. Immediately, my mother booked two tickets to Beirut for her and my dad, and although not originally planned, my sister and I accompanied them. About a week into our visit on Easter Sunday, my dad's mom, who was suffering from Alzheimer's, was taken to the hospital. Five days later on March 28, 2008 my dad's mom passed away.

A little over a week later, my mom's mother (who was the purpose of our trip) passed away from a disease called scleroderma. Within twelve days I had lost two of the most important people in my life. I became very angry with God. I stopped believing in him. I didn't think that it was fair for me to believe God existed. Why would God take away my grandmothers when I only got to see them once a year? I was only 14 years old. I didn't have enough time to get to know them before they were gone. So, I gave up on God. I stopped praying every night before bed. I felt God had betrayed me, so therefore he didn't deserve my faith.

For two years after my grandmothers' deaths, I didn't go to church. One Sunday morning, I woke up with a strong desire to turn back to God. So I went to Mass. It was at that Mass that I felt the overpowering love of the Holy Spirit. As St. Augustine said, "Our heart is restless until it rests in you O Lord." I experienced a sense of peace that my heart was yearning for.

I can't say that I wasn't scared to start believing in God again. In fact, it was the scariest thing I've ever done. I'm still scared. I'm scared that even if I trust him, believe in him, and stand up for him, I'll be let down again. But, that's life and there are always going to be ups and downs. It's during the difficult times that I know God is there for me the most, and that I will never, ever, be alone.

The Spirit Whispered: Rest assured my child, I will consistently love you no matter what. I am there to ease the pain. Times like this are difficult, but I will be there to hold your hand, ease your sorrow, and continue to guide you on your journey.

Prayer: Divine Spirit, help me to trust and believe in you. Deepen my faith in you when I feel all hope is lost. Give me strength during the most difficult situations, and help me to know that I am never alone, for you are always by my side.

Tracey Jabbour, *Mathematics and Statistics*
Novi, MI

Whisper Thirty-Seven: He Thirsts For Us

I have always struggled with letting myself be vulnerable when it comes to God. I grew up in a very Catholic household and went to church every Sunday and every holy day of obligation, although I was simply going through the motions. I didn't take the time to work on my personal relationship with God, and just let myself continue to coast through my daily routine. Then last year, my grandma sent me, and the rest of her grandchildren, a copy of "I Thirst for You," a meditation that has been attributed to Mother Theresa. It sat on my desk for a couple days, maybe almost a week, before I decided to read it, and I am so happy I did.

The words were so powerful, more powerful than I had expected them to be. I remember sitting in bed reading in silence, and just letting the tears stream down my face, letting my heart be open to God's voice. I was so touched by these words, and I knew the Spirit was working through each word and all the emotions I was feeling to help me realize how immensely profound his love for me is.

She sent it again this year. I know if I need encouragement, I can open it up and let his words speak to me. Even as I look over it now, I get teary-eyed. I have finally come to the realization that God loves me more than I can even begin to understand, and that blows my mind. I can now say I have a much better relationship with God, and even though it is nowhere near perfect, it is something I am constantly working on because I know just how important that relationship is.

The Spirit Whispered: I know you better than anyone. When you call I will answer. I love you just as you are, no matter what you do. I thirst for you always.

Prayer: Divine Spirit, your love is truly above anything we can comprehend. Help us open the eyes of our heart and truly see you.

This prayer, "I Thirst for You," by Mother Teresa is powerful. Here is just the end of the prayer:

"...Whenever you do open the door of your heart, whenever you come close enough, you will hear me say to you again and again, not in mere human words but in spirit. No matter what you have done, I love you for your own sake. Come to me with your misery and your sins, with your troubles and needs, and with all your longing to be loved. I stand at the door of your heart and knock. Open to me, for I THIRST FOR YOU..."

Bridgitte Laffrey, *Spanish Major*
Rockford, MI

"Difficulties come when we don't
pay attention to life's whisper.
Life always whispers to you first,
but if you ignore the whisper,
sooner or later
you will get a scream."

Oprah Winfrey

Whisper Thirty-Eight: Let it Be

Like many other Spartan Catholics, I can be labeled as a "Cradle Catholic," or in other words, someone who was born into a Catholic family, baptized as a baby, and raised in the Catholic faith. For us, Catholicism is all we've ever known.

Growing up my parents took me to church on Sundays, enrolled me in weekly catechism classes, and I was constantly reminded of holy sacraments: Baptism, Communion, Reconciliation, Confirmation, and then, one day, Holy Matrimony. I enjoyed attending Mass singing. I also loved seeing friends at catechism, where we analyzed readings and completed activities in our booklets. I was proud of my faith, and I couldn't imagine life without it. Like I said Catholicism is all I'd ever known.

During the eighth grade, I was officially confirmed within the Catholic Church alongside my peers at St. Patrick's Catholic Church of Brighton, Michigan. Shortly after I was confirmed, I began high school. High school was a new beast, one I wasn't quite as prepared to tackle as I thought. The teachers held higher expectations, the courses were more challenging, and friend circles shifted. Some of my childhood friends, the ones I pictured attending college with me, and one day standing up in my wedding, were no longer in my life. I was in a new school, finally combined with the students from our middle school, with minimal true friends, all while I was taking a load of strenuous classes. I felt like a single guppy in the ocean: alone and overwhelmed in the big world.

My parents believed a solid solution to my struggles at school would be to sign me up for a high school youth group that met on a weekly basis. At this point in my life, I was really questioning my faith. Priests always declared that God's intended plans would lead us to happiness, and that we should allow him to hold our fates in the palms of His hands. I would look at those around me and think to myself, "Why does everyone else seem happier than I am? Does God love them more than he loves me?" I struggled grasping the concept of one God controlling the lives of billions of people around the globe, yet I was still feeling empty.

109

At the time, I was in a complete rage about my parents forcing me to attend youth group. I was positive that I would be an outcast, that I wouldn't make friends, and that I wouldn't have a good time. Well, spoiler alert, I was severely wrong.

I looked forward to going every Sunday evening to see my new friends, to grow closer in my faith, and to get to see Glenna, who was our director of youth ministry through the parish. She delivered information in a way that was exciting and relatable, and she always planned fun activities. If we were in need of counsel, she listened and offered advice. If we were hungry, she fed us. If we behaved in a way that was un-Christian, she prayed for us. If we were upset, she hugged us. And if we needed friendship, she was there for us. She was a very important and influential woman in all of our lives, and in more ways than one, she saved us all.

In November 2011, I attended The National Catholic Youth Conference, also known as NCYC, which was hosted at Lucas Oil Stadium in Indianapolis, Indiana. This was a weekend-long conference which was a mixture of mingling, prayer, praise, worship, music, song, and self-discovery with 25,000 fellow high school students from all 50 states. A group of students from my parish and I rode down in a charter bus and stayed in a hotel that was designated for everyone from Michigan. We got the chance to meet lots of great people, some who lived very close to us, that we didn't even know existed! Aside from making new friends, I also got to know the members from my own parish even better than before. We shared faith-filled stories, giggled about jokes on the bus, and we bonded over never-ending boxes of pizza.

One of the nights at the conference we went to an upbeat, music-based praise and worship program in Lucas Oil Stadium, which included a teenage girl's vocal rendition of "Let It Be" by The Beatles. I remember it to this day, clear as ever, standing there in the stadium, singing along to the lyrics, when all of a sudden the song just spoke to me. It was incredible to look around the stadium and see 25,000 other teenagers on fire with their faith, leaving their emotional baggage at home and embracing the opportunity with full-force. An overwhelming feeling came over me, almost as a sense of relief. The girl's singing was so pure and true as she sang, "When I find myself in times of trouble, Mother Mary comes to me speaking words of wisdom: let it be." It was as if Mother Mary, in the flesh, took over the girl's body, and was speaking to me heart-to-heart. A few lines later, she sang "There will be an answer, let it be." Disbelief, fear, anxiety, stress, and all other emotions involving school and my social life instantly vanished.

When I look back at photos on Facebook of NCYC, it's not just a conference I attended. It's the glue that brought my "Cradle Catholic" views together with my present-day views. I would truly call it a life-changing experience. If it wasn't for NCYC, I wouldn't have kept the flame of my faith burning bright all throughout high school and wouldn't continue to grow in my faith at Michigan State University.

The Spirit Whispered: Do not worry about the present, "There will be an answer, let it be."

Prayer: Divine Spirit, help me to learn not to fret the small things, but to instead live my life according to your will. Guide me on my journey of trusting you, and better reassure me that everything is part of God's plan.

Danielle Campbell, *Creative Advertising*
Howell, MI

"Let your heart guide you.
It whispers,
so listen carefully."

Stu Krieger

Whisper Thirty-Nine: What Do You Want Me To Do For You?

All my life I have been striving to be like others, to try and earn my parents' love. One of my friends in middle school got the best grades by barely even studying. It drove me crazy, because I automatically set that goal for myself to be like her. Because I saw her natural smartness as perfection, I set being like her as a goal I was striving for. But having a supposed "perfect" friend really wasn't the source of my problem. My problem was this: I thought love had to be earned. I thought that if I was perfect, I would receive more attention and more love from my family and teachers. I would bring back a test or do well in a dance recital and I would receive a hug and my parents would look at me with that look in their eyes like: "Wow, honey I am so proud of you." And, I equated that with love. Therefore, when I saw others doing a better job than me, I thought to myself, "I can do better. Then I will receive more attention. Then I will receive more love."

Then, my parent's got a divorce. I blamed myself. I kept thinking that if only I had been a more perfect daughter, a better sister, a better person, that they might have not split up. I started to doubt that God cared for me. It didn't make sense that he would let this happen to us. I tried being a perfect daughter, listening and agreeing with both of my parents, which caused me even more confusion because I tried choosing sides. I thought I could somehow fix our family. I began to sink into depression. Every night I would cry myself to sleep, wondering if our family would ever be healed. Then one night, as I was crying myself to sleep, I started praying again. My prayer was this: "If everything that everybody says about you is true, Father, take this weight from me. I can't fix my family. So I give this burden to you." At that moment, I was filled with a peace that I had never felt before, and I stopped crying. Immediately I knew that God was real, that he loved me with a personal love that I couldn't fathom, and that I didn't have to carry that burden any longer. I felt as if I was his alone, and no one could separate me from him. It was as if an enormous weight was lifted from my chest, and I could finally breathe again. In Psalm 23, the psalmist writes, "Even though I walk through the valley of the shadow of death, I fear no evil; for thou art with me; thy rod and thy staff they comfort me." I was walking through that dreaded valley, and for the first time I did not fear the evil, because God's presence overwhelmed me.

After God broke into my life and relieved my self-inflicted burden of healing my family, I did not immediately respond. I actually sinned the most consistently right after this. But now looking back, I know that each time I was sinning, Jesus was looking at me with a gaze of pure love, calling me to come back to him. I just refused to listen. I wanted to make my own destiny, turn myself into the person I wanted to be. I had no idea that God had a better plan for my life. I was oblivious to the fact that God created me to be someone and to have a purpose in his plan of love. Through God's grace alone, I did finally get out of the pit of sin I started after that night. I was then trying to be a "good person," and I knew that I wanted something more than the life I had, but I didn't turn directly to God. He would draw me to himself for a while with prayer meetings and friends who had amazing faith, but I would always turn away from him eventually.

Luckily, God is constantly pursuing us, and longing to give us the life he planned for us. Through a series of events that only could have occurred through divine providence, I went on a retreat my junior year of high school with the youth group at my parish. My pastor was leading the retreat. One of the passages that we were reflecting on throughout the weekend was Mark 10:46-52. This passage describes the blind man Bartimaeus shouting from the ditch: "Jesus, Son of David, have mercy on me!" Jesus stops and asks, "What do you want me to do for you?" As I reflected on this, I kept thinking my response would be something to the effect of, "Tell me I am on the right path in my life."

Later on the retreat, we had confession. After I confessed my sins, my pastor asked me, "If Jesus was physically standing in front of you, and asked, "What do you want me to do for you, Monica? What would you say?" I blurted out: "I want you to heal my parents." Not exactly what I planned. But that is exactly what I needed to say. Father then responded with asking me to think about the cross. To anyone passing Calvary, Jesus looked defeated. He looked done for. But, on that third day, he was gloriously risen. He conquered sin and death by his gruesome self-sacrifice. God has an unexpected and amazing way of turning trash into gold. He wants to do that in my life, in my relationships, and my family. He wants to do this in all of our lives. After this discussion, I felt that same peace I had experienced before. I finally gave my shattered, broken life to the Lord, and asked him to transform it like he transformed his death, according to his will, not mine.

My life has never been the same. I have never felt more peaceful, free, or loved. And I have no idea what plans God has in store for me. All I know is that I try each day to give all of my life to God. He is now the reason I get up in the morning. He is the reason why I am at Michigan State. Over the years, God has drawn me deeper and deeper into an awesome friendship. I'm not going to lie and say that I feel like this every day. However, God gives me the grace to keep trying. He gives me the grace to make those choices that lead me to the person that I was created to be.

The Spirit Whispered: I love you more than you could ever imagine. I am with you always, even in the valley. I want to transform your life, and give you a future and hope.

Prayer: Divine Spirit, help me to truly know that your love is infinitely more that I could ever imagine. You look upon us, weak sinners, with unfathomable love. Spirit, help me respond to that love. Give me unshakable joy in the midst of the chaos and unshakeable peace of knowing who I am to you, and where I am supposed to be.

Monica Wegienka, *Zoology and Pre-Vet Studies*
Canton, MI

"When the world says,
'Give up,'
Hope whispers,
'Try it one more time.'"

Hannah Miles

Whisper Forty: Building Bridges

After over a year of waiting, a Michigan family traveled across the world to Romania to meet the little girl they would bring back with them, with the little information they had been given, her name, a picture, and that she was very talkative. A mother and daughter loved that little girl, Geanina, with all their hearts. Meanwhile, while I was in the orphanage, I was unaware how deeply these two people loved me, I was unaware of how much God cared about me, and I didn't like my name, Geanina.

Having been born into extreme poverty, placed into an orphanage where no child deserves to live for five years, and lacking a loving father figure once I was adopted, I didn't realize how much I was truly cared for until I learned about developing a personal relationship with God. I didn't know about his unconditional love for me and his ultimate kindness. Recently I learned that "Geanina" means "God is gracious" or "God is kind" and "God's Gift." It was then that my attitude about my name changed.

Appropriately, through all my troubles, my challenges, and my joys, God has used significant people in my life to express his kindness. Life was not automatically care-free and pleasant after being adopted, but I had wonderful support. After my arrival to a brand new home, with new people, in a very new culture, I was naturally distressed. Scared of the unknown, scared of being "sent back" to the orphanage, and untrained in "proper" social skills, I was in desperate need of some tender loving care. Knowing this, God provided for me two of the strongest women I know to love me. My mother took her time to let me bond with her, and to nurture me the best she could. My sister, despite my initial negativity towards her, reached out to love me. She was my caregiver when my mom was working, and my protector. Through the years, our family relationships have been tested extensively, and I have learned to appreciate how much I love these women God put into my life, how much they love me, and that God loves me even more than I can imagine.

If you've ever traveled anywhere, you've probably encountered a bridge of some sort. Bridges do not "erase" an obstacle, they make it possible or easier to overcome the obstacle. Being the kind and merciful Lord that he is, God has provided many bridges, in the form of people, opportunities, and those events, big or small that make me smile. Besides my mother and sister, I've encountered God's compassion through people who've showed me kindness and understanding. Each time my mom was in the hospital for major surgery over the course of ten years, we had family friends praying, inviting us to come, and offering support. After having a very poor experience with teachers in elementary school, I moved into a new district in time to have a few of the best teachers I could ever ask for in fifth grade. Though I could not "replace" the best friend I lost in high school, I have met several new friends and become closer to other friends, who I could share my faith with.

God helps me build bridges as I approach the deepest of waters. He may not always give me what I want, but he has given me what I need. I'm a Michigan State University student because God gave me an opportunity I didn't want at the time. After losing a big scholarship to Central Michigan University, and finding out at the orientation that I would not be able to attend in the fall, all my failures went rushing through my mind. The thought of missing the required 3.8 GPA by less than .5 reminded me of all the times I had come "so close" to my goal, but failed. What didn't go through my mind was how far I have come since arriving in the States, and everything God had given me to put me where I was.

Remember that talkative little girl in the orphanage? Talking was God's way of helping me cope, survive, and perhaps even keep my sanity. I remember how much heartache I went through, wanting a loving father because God gave me the desire to love and be loved. I remember how much I went through trying to be kind to others, because God has been so kind to me, in part through other people. My name is a reminder to me now of God as the ultimate source of kindness.

Since I can remember, I've tried hard to be "lovable," not realizing how much I was loved unconditionally. I've wanted to be smart in school, so much that I cheated on timed math tests in elementary. I wanted my teachers to like me, and was terrified of letting them down by not doing well. I wanted my parents to love me for the things I did, not knowing that my father would never be able to, but my mother already did love me with all her heart. I've tried and tried, but nothing I do can make God love me any more than he does.

Long before I can remember he has planned the right moments, and the places for me to be. And even the moments I may not remember have an impact on me. During a recent discussion with my mom, I was practically offended when she brought up the idea of the orphanage affecting who I am today. I don't have any more clear memories of the first five years- and I thought I had "gotten over" any problems I brought. But like any mother, she was right. Nobody can just get "over" an experience like that, it takes work to get "through" these times. While I don't remember it, that experience will always be a part of me, just like the other big events in my life. I wasn't even present for the ultimate sacrifice- the ultimate demonstration of kindness, and the sacrifice Jesus made for us. Because of that, I know I am loved, and God's love and kindness is the biggest, strongest bridge he could ever build for me.

The Spirit Whispered: Have faith in the Lord, and he will take care of you. Let him love you.

Prayer: Divine Spirit, who is kind and merciful, help me to love myself as you love me, and to spread your love throughout the world.

Geanina Luis, *Neuroscience and Education*
East Lansing MI

"None of us will ever accomplish
anything excellent
or commanding except when
one listens
to this whisper
which is heard by that one person alone."

Thomas Carlyle

Whisper Forty-One: A Life of Faith

My roommate Danny may not seem like the type to those who only casually know him, but, as someone who has known him for 15 years, he has deep faith and inspires others. Other people have said that he has a great gift for sharing his experiences. What he has to say really makes them think. Danny is a great friend and person to be around. Coming from someone who knows him well, this is all true, but there's more to him than that.

Anyone who's smelled the microwave in our apartment immediately recognizes two smells: hot dogs and chili. Why is this? Danny loves chili dogs. As such, it was no accident that this is what he chose to give up for Lent this year. This seems trivial to anyone who doesn't know him well, but this is 46 straight days he went without one of his favorite meals. His older brother found out he gave up his chili dogs. His brother sincerely said, "Danny is a religious person."

Knowing Danny and how much it took for him to do this was a sacrifice. I went to a Catholic school for 14 years, so I see this clearly as a great sacrifice. That wasn't the only sacrifice he made.

There's no disputing the fact Danny is the number one Detroit Tigers fan. Three out of the last four years, he watched every single game of the season. That's at least 162 games a year. This past year, the Tigers qualified for the playoffs, but there was an issue. The first round of the playoffs was during St. John's fall retreat. He made it very clear that he didn't want to go on the retreat. However, he chose his faith over his favorite team. I like to think that Christ inspired him to go on the retreat knowing that he'd be able to reach out to others.

One of the speakers on the retreat, a good friend of ours, said that it's the little things that make the greatest difference. Danny took this to heart and, when he saw someone sitting alone during free time, he did the simple act of sitting with her and talking to her. It seems frivolous to us, but to this lonely girl, it made her feel so welcome in our community. Following that, in his retreat small group, he said that we'd have no direction in life without our faith. Let me tell you, he clearly has direction in his life. You can even find him at daily Mass.

Think about it, how many college students do you know who go to Mass more than once a week? In today's society, that's far from ordinary.

Father Mark, the pastor of St. John's, has a great sense of humor. He uses humor to communicate powerful messages. One of his better known uses of this is when he uses a play on words to talk about the difference between "Big S" and Little "s" saints. He may never get that St. Title next to his name, but he definitely has the qualities of becoming one. Men like him are hard to come by, but, if you know where to look, just might meet one who could be hiding in plain sight.

The Spirit Whispered: Without faith, we'd have no direction in life. We need God in our lives to live a meaningful life.

Prayer: Divine Spirit, help us to always be strong especially when we want to do those things that will help us to be a better person of faith.

Chris Shim, *Arts and Humanities and Spanish*
Canton, MI

Whisper Forty-Two: Leaving Something You Love

My mother says she always knew that I was going to be a tennis player, because even when I was two years old, I walked around the house hitting a plastic golf ball with a pen. My mother was right; by age three I was out on the tennis court hitting balls around with my dad, and at five I started to take lessons. My competitive play began at the age of eight with Rookie Tour Tournaments for kids 10 and under; I was so excited and nervous to play in my first tournament. I did not win a trophy, which disappointed me at the time, but it made me even more determined to practice more. The next year I won two out of the three tournaments on the Rookie Tour and I finished second in the one I did not win. These couple of years sparked a love that I had for the sport that continued for many years.

As I got older, my love for tennis continued and my skill level steadily increased. At 13 years old, I was a scrawny and quiet freshman on the tennis team at Lansing Catholic High School (LCHS). My coach and future Confirmation sponsor, Ron Landfair, played a huge impact on my life through my tennis game as well as my faith. In my four years of high school, he led the team to two state runner-up finishes and he helped me win a Division 4 state title at number one singles. As high school began to wrap up, I contemplated playing tennis at the college level. Some Division, three coaches contacted me, but I didn't want to attend any of their schools. Academics always came first for me, so I decided to attend Michigan State University.

I did not believe I could play tennis for a Division I school until Coach Gene Orlando, the head coach of the Michigan State University team, came to one of my practices over the summer between high school and college and told my dad that he liked what he saw. This conversation inspired me to work extremely hard and, through the grace of God, coach Gene Orlando took a chance on me, adding me to the last spot on the roster even after I failed to win a single challenge match at tryouts. My freshman year on the team was an amazing experience as my teammates and I were the first team in school history to make it to the NCAA tournament. Even though we lost in the first round, this achievement was a huge step forward for the program.

When my sophomore year rolled around, we struggled as a team. We could not find an identity and had a hard time meshing and working together. Because of these struggles, I did not enjoy my time on the team as much that year as I had the previous year. Also, in March, I found out that I had a micro-tear in my labrum, the cartilage between two bones in my right shoulder. The doctors at Michigan State said that I did not need surgery as long as I could deal with the pain, so I went to physical therapy in an attempt to heal myself. As the season came to a close, we failed to make the NCAA tournament, and, sadly, I had to say goodbye to my best friend on the team, Aaron Pfister, as he graduated and began life in the working world.

Junior year started off really strong for us as we made it a point to come together as a team. Damian Hume, the assistant coach of the team, aided in this unity by planning an awesome team retreat to the Sleeping Bear Dunes in northern Michigan. We were a lot closer as a team and this showed in our results as we compiled more wins in the fall tournaments than the previous two years. My shoulder was getting marginally better as I was slowly starting to be able to practice more than I had in the last four months. Winter break started and I was pretty excited for the season to start. However, as I hit more over the three-week period before the team was to start practicing together, my shoulder started to feel worse and worse. I could hardly hit a serve without pain, I had to take breaks during hitting sessions, and I had to take more days off than I wanted to in order to rest my weary shoulder. As the time came for the team to start returning from vacation, I told my girlfriend, Elizabeth Hillman, that I was not enjoying tennis as much as usual, and I brought up the fact that I was not very excited to start the season. She said, "If you don't enjoy it then why are you still doing it?" The question rocked me to my core, so I started to think about it, and I could not come up with a great answer. My thought process was, "Well, it's tennis, and I've always done it." After wrapping up our conversation, I realized that I lost the love and passion that I once had for the game that made me want to work hard and help the team out in any way I could.

The team met for an unofficial practice and afterwards went to an MSU basketball game. I could not focus during either of these two events as I struggled to decide what to do with my future. That night, I talked to Damian, my parents, and Elizabeth about what I was struggling with. Before I went to bed, I prayed to God asking for help with this struggle. Though he did not answer me directly, he helped me to realize that I was going to make the right decision.

The next day, I told Coach Orlando what I had been contemplating. He told me that it was my call. On January 6, 2015, I broke the news to my teammates that I decided to quit the team because I didn't have passion for the sport and I was sick of being injured all the time.

When I told the team of my decision, they were all very supportive and said very kind words. As I sat in the locker room, my mind started to race as I wondered what I was going to do with my life now that one of the most important and integral parts of my life was over. I decided one of the best ways to use the extra time I had was to get more involved at St. John Church and Student Center. I had always gone to Mass every Sunday; thanks to Coach Orlando I was able to go even when the tennis team traveled to away matches. However, Mass had been the extent of my church involvement. I hadn't attended the Men's Group at the church since early in my freshmen year of college; after attending a meeting in the first few weeks of school, I felt more at home than I had in years. The guys made me feel welcome by inviting me to snow football, pick-up basketball, and the Spring Retreat. Since I had not gone on retreat since my senior year of high school, I made up my mind at the last minute to attend the retreat. I felt like my faith could get stronger and that I would try to "Encounter God." I was blessed to experience the Lord through awesome talks from the retreat leaders, getting to know the people in my small group, meeting up with old friends and making new ones.

It has been seven weeks since I made up my mind to let go of one of the greatest parts of my life. I thank the Lord for gracing me with the strength to go through with the decision because the beginning of this semester has been an amazing and faith-filled experience. It hasn't all been sunshine and roses, but I have been able to spend more time with friends, play other sports, and, as I mentioned above, become more involved in the church. As I conclude my story, I want to finish with a quote that my mom gave to me on a bookmark the day after my big decision. It said, "But I have noticed that during the most trying periods of my life there has only been one set of footprints in the sand. Why, when I needed you most, have you not been there for me?" The Lord replied, "The years when you have seen only one set of footprints, my child, is when I carried you."

The Spirit Whispered: God helped me to realize that it was time to leave the competitive tennis world and to start making him a more centralized aspect of my life.

Prayer: Divine Spirit, thank you for blessing me with many talents over the course of my life and for helping me to realize when it is time to move on with my life. I ask for your blessing as I move forward and look to make my faith a greater part of my life.

Paul Heeder, *Mechanical Engineering*
East Lansing, MI

Whisper Forty-Three: My Grandpa Truly Inspired Me

There is a very famous saying that I'm sure you've heard before: "be careful what you wish for." This past Christmas, I wished for something that I thought would make me happier and better. I was waiting to meet with my friend who was going to the movies with me. Since she was running extremely late, instead of getting upset, I decided to do something kind. I bought our tickets and decided this would be a nice little Christmas present for her. I asked God to help me remember the true meaning of Christmas and I wanted to grow in our relationship. I plan to reach out and do kind deeds for others. When I got home, I cleaned the dishes in the sink, so my parents wouldn't have to deal with them in the morning and basically I was on a cheery holiday roll.

The next morning, we went to my grandma's for Christmas Eve brunch. With only one day till Christmas, I was really excited to be with my family. We all gathered for breakfast, said our prayer, and began to eat. Everyone was there except for my Papa. At 73, he was off playing in a hockey game and would be showing up later after the meal was over. Halfway through breakfast, there was a phone call, my grandma went to answer it. My papa said that he wasn't feeling well and that a friend of his called an ambulance to come pick him up, mostly as a precaution. My dad and grandma went to meet him at the hospital. We finished breakfast, sure that in a few hours he would be back home.

It was that day my grandpa suffered three heart attacks. There were multiple times that we were called back to see him. The doctors were very certain that he wouldn't make it through the heart attack. Each heart attack that occurred scared my family. We were filled with fear because we didn't know what was going to happen. The healthiest man I knew was dying. Here it is Christmas Eve, and my family was praying for nothing short of a Christmas miracle.

You never realize how much love you have in your life until your family suffers a tragedy. For the next seven days that my grandpa remained in the ICU, my family received multiple visits from my priest and my grandma's pastor. There were many cards, flowers, and phone calls from family and friends. Seeing this display of kind gestures would bring us to tears. I am convinced that all the prayers is what saved my grandpa. On Christmas Day he woke up. The day after Christmas he was talking and watching sports. That weekend my uncle from Texas came up and spent all day just talking to my grandpa and watching him sleep. The following Monday he was transported to another hospital for a minor surgery. He was laughing and walking and was completely him. Nothing had changed, he was the grandpa that I had always known. The grandpa that lived a mile from me my whole life and was like a second dad. The grandpa who went to Vegas to play in a national softball tournament that previous October and had also refereed three to four basketball games a week. The one that walked our dog every day and came over 'just because' multiple times a week. By the grace of God and through countless prayers, my grandpa had survived the worst. Surely, we received our miracle.

The day after his minor surgery, I was to leave for Florida for a vacation with my boyfriend. Because of the events of the prior week I wanted to ask my grandpa's permission to go. If needed, I had no problem delaying the trip a few days. For just a few hours after I was to leave, he would be going home and starting his road to recovery, and I knew that my family would need all the help they could get. When I told my grandpa that I was considering staying home rather than going to Florida, he brushed the idea away immediately. He promised that I wouldn't be needed at home and that we would catch up when I got back. As I said my goodbyes, I leaned down to kiss his forehead and he told me, "I love you, and I promise that we will have plenty more times together." I walked out the door and had no idea that these would be the last words my grandpa would ever speak to me.

Tuesday, December 30, 2014 will forever be one of the darkest days of my life. It is the day that my papa left this earth and all his loved ones behind. I was angry with God.

I couldn't stop asking questions. Why did it happen the day I left for Florida? Why wasn't I home with my family? Why did he have to have another heart attack as soon as he got home when he was essentially healthy the last few days at the hospital? Why him? Why did he tell me we would have plenty of time? Did he not know? Why did he survive all that time in the hospital if he was just going to die the whole time? Why didn't it just happen on Christmas Eve?

I started to question my faith. But in the days that followed his death, I began getting insights into some of the questions I wanted answers to. My grandpa was so loved. There were over 370 people who show up for both his visitation and funeral.

Every person came with a story. My grandpa was an extremely modest man; and apparently, incredibly generous, kind, and to some a surprise. This man devoted his life to God. Left and right people began telling me stories of how my grandpa would clean out his closet to give clothes to his students at the Detroit school he worked at. At Thanksgiving and Christmas, he bought turkeys and delivered them door to door to some of the families in his school. He changed so many people's lives and encouraged people to pursue their dreams. His refereeing friends told me that he was the reason they started to be referees in the first place. Teachers and counselors shared how he inspired them to pursue their careers. My grandpa may have been Detroit's most loved man and because of his humility, none of us had any idea. However, in his last few days, he decided to re-dedicate his life to God. In a conversation with my mom, he admitted that he had been cheating life and that God had given him a second chance to really live life the way he was meant to. Those final days in the hospital may have been just enough to save his soul.

If you would have asked me before Christmas Eve what a Christmas miracle is, I promise you that my answer would be a whole lot different than it is now. We all know the story of Christmas; however, the true miracle lies in the fact that Jesus saves us and he saved my grandpa by allowing him a few extra days to make his peace and tell his family that he loved us. Jesus didn't just save my grandpa's soul. He saved so many more. My grandpa influenced and inspired as many people in his death as in his life. As for me, I can honestly say that I am changed from the inside out. I am inspired to live my life for others, and mostly, for God. To give my life to help those in need, to share the gifts I have been given, and to go to sleep every night knowing that I made the world a little better than it was when I woke up that morning. I had to share my grandpa's story. He was an incredible man who lived his life in the way that God asks us to, to give our time and talents to help those around us. Through the death of my grandpa, I have opened my eyes and my heart to what God asks of me. God wants me to live my life to the fullest. Every single day is a gift from God. I received my Christmas miracle, and I receive it every day that I am able to serve him. I want to dedicate this story my grandpa, Joseph A. Kavulich.

The Spirit Whispered: Always live your life in a way that inspires others to be all that they can be.

Prayer: Divine Spirit, please help me to always remember that every day is a gift from God with a purpose. Remind me to live my life in a way that brings me closer to my purpose.

Kara Kavulich, *Elementary Education*
Plymouth, MI

Whisper Forty-Four: Following God's Plan

Coming to Michigan State University was probably one of the biggest changes in my life. Although I was scared and nervous, I really wanted a fresh start outside of my comfort zone. I was getting excited to come during the summer, and once I found out who my roommate was, it made it even better. We started talking, and I found out we had quite a bit in common. Then, two days before move-in day, my roommate decided she was going to live at home.

All I could think about was how I would be all alone in a new place with no friends. Even though everyone was telling me that everything would work out, I was still completely scared. Then, move-in day came along, and everything was going okay. My family came and helped me settle in, but I still did not have a roommate or even a friend.

Once my family left, I was a mess. I think I called my mom at least once a day during the first week. I was talking to new people, but I still felt so alone. Then on the first day of classes, I went to get lunch. While I was eating, a girl came up to me, and asked if she could sit next to me because she didn't want to sit alone. I said "sure," and we started talking about classes, majors, family, where we were from, and all of the basic things freshmen talk to each other about. Our conversation continued, and we somehow started talking about St. John's. She asked if I was Catholic, and when I told her I was, she invited me to come to Thursday night Mass with her and her roommate.

I believe that it was in God's plan that I had no roommate my first semester at Michigan State University, so I was able to meet some of my best friends. Without meeting these people, I probably would not be as involved in St. John's as I am today, and would not have met such wonderful people.

131

The Spirit Whispered: Be patient. You will meet some new friends and your relationship with me will flourish.

Prayer: Divine Spirit, help all those who feel alone in this world. Let them know that you are with them through the good and the bad.

Kelly Weingartz, *Chemistry*
Macomb, MI

"Believe in yourself and all that you are.
Know there is something inside you that
greater than any obstacle."

Christian D. Larson

Whisper Forty-Five: The Blessing within My Curse

The summer sun shone brightly as I walked back from the forest with my sister and cousin, our arms full of branches for our chalet. Suddenly, a searing pain, something that felt like a lightning bolt shot through my hip. I remember dropping the branches. I remember running straight down the road all the way back to my cottage. I remember the tears streaming down my cheeks as the pain would not give way. I remember lying down on my back on my grandmother's bed, the whole family crowding around me trying to figure out what was wrong. I was only six.

As the years passed, I had little bolts shoot through my hip countless times. Sometimes it was a couple times a day, other times once in a month. Doctor after doctor waived it off saying, "If you've had it that long, it can't be serious." "Maybe it'll pass?" No one could tell me what the lightning bolts were, no one could tell me why I was the one having them, no one understood. As far as I was concerned, I was cursed, bound to live my life helplessly with mysterious lightning bolts running through my hip at their own whim.

I was a freshman in college when one of my professors asked us to interview our parents about our births. I heard all the "normal stuff" that I had already known: how much I weighed, how red I was, that I was somewhat premature, and what book my mom had been reading just before she delivered me. It had been 13 years since my first lightning bolt struck. The interview was almost done when my mom suddenly remembered something. Very nonchalantly, she added, "Oh yeah, the doctor said you were lucky. Your neural tube had closed just in time." I pried, searching for more information, but that was all the doctor had said, that was all she knew. That's when I heard the Holy Spirit, that's when I felt in my heart that I knew the answer. "It's a blessing, not a curse. I love you; I always have."

I'd learned about the neural tube a few times in my classes. I knew it was a fetal organ that eventually developed into the brain and spinal cord. But I never thought that my hip pain could be a result of

135

something that happened before I was born. Soon enough the answer was on my computer screen: Spina Bifida Occulta. My undiagnosed curse was actually a blessing.

Had it been the other end of my neural tube, I would've lived for a matter of weeks. Had my neural tube closed a few days later, I might have been paralyzed from the waist down. I could have had a pouch of spinal fluid poking out of my back, unprotected. All I had was a slightly weak leg and a few sporadic lightning bolts shooting through my hip. What I had was tangible proof of what a doctor had called luck, but the Holy Spirit called love.

The Spirit Whispered: It's a blessing, not a curse. I love you, I always have.

Prayer: Divine Spirit, Help me to see the blessings bestowed upon me amidst life's adversities. Amen.

Agnieszka Felczak, *Child Development*
Warsaw, Poland

Whisper Forty-Six: My Church and My Career

I did not start my college career as a Spartan; I used to be an Oakland University Grizzly. Many circumstances led me to leave Oakland after my freshman year and Michigan State seemed to be the logical choice since my sister was a student there and with my parent's help, we bought a house just off campus. Honestly, I was not very happy to be transferring to such a huge school. I decided to spend my freshman year spring break with my sister at Michigan State University to get a better feel of where I was heading. On Thursday night she took me to student Mass at St. John's and I fell in love. I knew right there that I wanted to be a part of this student community and I happily transferred to Michigan State.

During my first year here at MSU, I took part in many of St. John Student Center's activities. My favorite being the Undergraduate Retreats. At the end of the year, Sr. Dorothy was looking for students to lead the next year's fall retreat and I decided to be a part of that. Back then, I had no idea how important that decision would be to my future.

Starting my junior year, I realized how important internships are to getting a job after graduating, especially for a chemical engineer. I started researching companies and going to every networking and career fair I could. By the middle of spring semester there was only one engineering career fair left and I still had not gotten an internship. After blowing my chances with my top choice company due to extreme nerves, I decided to talk to the next company I saw no matter where they fell on my list. I turned the corner and the company at the first table was Consumers Energy. At first I wanted to walk past and go back to them later since they were pretty high on my list and I did not want to ruin my chances with them, but something told me to go for it.

After taking a deep breath, I went up to the table and handed the recruiter my resume. My mind was racing as she took some time to look at it. I was trying to prepare to give a more professional answer to her questions than I had at the last company. But nothing could have prepared me for her first question, "Where was the retreat you lead held?" The question confused me and I admitted that I could not remember the name of the place but that it was somewhere in DeWitt. She then asked if it was at Bethany House, and after I told her that it was she told me that she used to go to retreats there and was part of St. John's Student Center when she went to MSU and that she is now a parishioner there. We proceeded to have a conversation about church and our favorite priests and what sort of opportunities are offered to students now. I felt my nerves dissipate and by the time she started asking the normal interview questions I was relaxed and could answer each question with confidence.

Out of all the companies I had applied to, Consumers Energy was the only one to give me an interview. I am now preparing to start my second internship with them. I am hoping that I can impress them enough that they consider me for a full time job.

The Spirit Whispered: Trust me, and I will take care of you. I have a plan for you that is greater than your plan for yourself.

Prayer: Divine Spirit, thank you for everything you have given to me and all that you do in my life. Help me to use these gifts to better my life and the lives of those around me.

Allison Linder, *Chemical Engineering*
Westland MI

Whisper Forty-Seven: What Are You Waiting For?

It was 11:00 pm on a Wednesday night in late September after my first meeting with the Right of Christian Initiation for Adults [RCIA] director. The first person I wanted to call was my best friend, Geanina.

"You are going to be my sponsor," I said.

The excitement that I heard over the phone was deafening. I knew that she was excited for me. She had been waiting years for this. That night and in the months to follow, I had the opportunity to reflect on the moments leading up to the best decision of my life.
Growing up, my family wasn't religious. We believed in God and Jesus and we celebrated Christmas, but we never attended church. I had an idea of what Christianity was about, but I didn't have a spiritual relationship with God. I knew the facts but I didn't have a faith life. That all started to change when I attended Camp Barakel (a Christian summer camp) with a friend from elementary school. On July 27, 2005, while attending Camp Barakel, I accepted Jesus Christ as my Savior. I was on my way but there was a long journey ahead.

For years after, I still didn't live a spiritual life. I thought that since I had accepted Christ, I was done. Church was unnecessary and I only prayed to Jesus when I wanted something. I struggled most in my faith when I would go through difficult times in my life, whether it be family issues or even my grades in school. However, I quickly learned that God is not going to give me an "A" on a test, but rather the open mindedness to obtain the information needed and the attentiveness to sit down and study. Over the next seven years, Jesus was actively seeking me, and I thought I was doing the same. But the truth is I wasn't living a very Christian lifestyle. I put myself before others and I was still only praying to God when I wanted something. After a couple years and numerous struggles, I finally realized that having a relationship with Jesus Christ is a lifetime commitment, not just 10 minutes at camp. As I struggled to build my faith, my mother was losing hers. I loved Jesus and I wanted a relationship with him. My mom on the other hand had given up on the idea that God existed. We were on two different planets when it came to faith.

Throughout high school, my best friend kept encouraging me to come to church with her and to learn more about the Catholic faith. I went a few times just to make her happy. I didn't think any of it would benefit me. But lucky for me, Geanina wouldn't give up that easily. Towards the end of my sophomore year of high school, I became involved with a group called Campus Life. Campus Life was a Christ-centered youth group for middle school and high school teens. It was during Campus Life that I seriously started pursuing a relationship with Jesus Christ. I made so many incredible lifelong friends through Campus Life. My life had changed forever.

When I asked Geanina to be my RCIA sponsor, I had no idea what a huge impact the program would have on me. I learned things about the Catholic faith that I had never expected to learn. I fell in love with the faith and the church and I fell in love with the values and morals. I was finally understanding what it was like to have a relationship with Jesus and I couldn't have been happier. But then came another challenge. In January 2013, while in the middle of my RCIA program, both Geanina and my lives were turned upside down when a close family friend and neighbor passed away unexpectedly. We were devastated. We didn't know what we were going to do without this person in our lives. I believe that this situation pushed me further from God, but also brought me closer. I was distant for some time. I felt alone, but I quickly realized that I would never be alone, not with Jesus by my side. And for the first time in a very long time, I prayed. I prayed for her soul, I prayed for her husband, her family, and every one of her friends and family. Prayer helped me get through one of the toughest times in my life.

When you enter RCIA you are told that if you choose to continue with the process you will be Baptized, Confirmed and receive your First Holy Communion at the Easter Vigil, which takes place the night before Easter Sunday. All of my waiting was about to pay off as I walked into St. Thomas Aquinas on the night of the Easter Vigil. I was about to become a Catholic. A plethora of emotions was sweeping through me as the time came to be baptized into the Catholic faith. I was so excited, but at the same time I was nervous and unsure. But as I stepped into the pool and knelt down, all I could feel was happiness and love. As Fr. Mark baptized me, all I felt was peace and joy. The feeling continued as I was confirmed and received my First Holy Communion. I am now a Catholic!

It has been almost two years since becoming a Catholic. I cannot express how much joy I have felt in my heart and experienced in my life since I made the decision to join RCIA. Of course there have been difficulties, but I know now that I will never be left alone in situations where I am struggling. I will always have Jesus by my side. My faith has grown exponentially in the past two years, I have developed a closer relationship with Jesus and God the Father and I love going to Mass. Church is where I feel most at home. Even though my relationship with God is stronger than ever, I won't stop here. My journey is far from over.

The Spirit Whispered: The love of God will get you through any struggle or obstacle. Do not worry because the love of God will prevail.

Prayer: Divine Spirit, bless those who are struggling to find their faith and those who have strayed from their faith. May they always be aware of God's love.

Jamie McGrath, *Nursing*
East Lansing, MI

"We must make the world a place
where: love dominates our hearts,
nature sets the standard for beauty,
simplicity and honesty
are the essence
of our relationships,
kindness guides our actions
and everyone respects one another."

Susan Polis Schultz

Whisper Forty-Eight: A Guiding Hand

When we begin a new chapter in our life there are many challenges we face. Entering college is a new experience that comes with many challenges. When I began my freshman year, I was very anxious. I only knew two people at Michigan State and was over nine hours away from my home, family, and friends. Growing up in a very small town, this was the first time I was living in a place where everyone didn't know who I was and everything about me. It was a fresh start, but I didn't know where to begin. I felt lost in a sea of strangers and didn't know where to turn. I began attending St. John Church weekly and immediately felt comfortable being surrounded by so many passionate and positive people, and I felt like I had a new connection with God and others in the pew.

I always felt like I had a pretty good connection with God, but coming to college took that relationship to a whole new level. I would pray daily thanking him for everything he does and asking him for guidance in my daily life. When school was getting extra tough and I felt like I really needed extra guidance, I always felt like God was there to point me in the right direction and help me get through any troubles I had. No matter what troubles I was having, I always knew I could turn to God and he was going to be there for me. Whether it was being worried about an upcoming test, missing my family and friends back home, or struggles with friends here, he helped me to get through all the challenges I faced. He helped me to get through my freshman year and continues to assist me each and every day as a guiding hand that will always be at side.

The Spirit Whispered: You can do anything you set your mind to with my help. Turn to me in times of trouble. I will always be there for you.

Prayer: Divine Spirit, thank you for everything you do for all of us children. Please help us to work together to be full of faith, love and joy. Allow us to help each other to make this amazing world you have created the best it can possibly be.

Maighlin Kolesar, *Nutritional Sciences/Pre-med Major*
Ironwood, MI.

Pay attention to the whispers,

the nudges, the urgings.

Your soul is begging,

your life is waiting."

Author Unknown

Whisper Forty-Nine: Holy Pizza

The year was 2008. I had just begun my freshman year of high-school and there was an abundance of hormones raging within me. I had no clue what was going on around me and was quite honestly directionless in my life. I had just finished my middle-school career at St. Thomas Aquinas middle-school, in Ohio, but despite the school's best intentions, I was nowhere close to becoming a saint, let alone a practicing Catholic. I strongly disliked going to Mass and unfortunately did not want anything to do with the Church. Around this time is when God decided to step in and intervene.

The high school youth minster of St. Thomas at the time somehow managed to convince me to come to one of the youth group events. In reality one of the only reasons I went to the event was because it was a paintball outing and I figured a chance to shoot other people would be pretty cool. The event went well; however, I still was hesitant to accept the youth minister's persistence inviting me back to the weekly youth group meetings. However, little did I know, the Holy Spirit was about to work in me and make me think otherwise. After one particular invite from the youth minister and a fellow peer the Spirit whispered *"Ryan, you really should go to the youth group meeting this week."*

I tried to ignore the quiet peaceful voice in my head by brushing it off and convincing myself the meeting would be boring. This did not work as well as I thought it would once my friend and the youth minister brought up the fact that there would be pizza at that meeting. I finally decided to go almost entirely because there would be pizza. I haven't looked back since.

After that first time, I never missed another youth group meeting that my former youth minister led and I am blessed to be able to say that I am now currently helping out with this youth group as a college volunteer.

The Spirit Whispered: Ryan, you really should go to this youth group meeting this week!

Prayer: Divine Spirit, lead me to where you are calling me. Show me what you want me to do with my life and help me to surrender every aspect of my life into your hands. I know the fact that I am trying to do your will does not mean that I am always doing so, but I trust in you. Help me to overlook my imperfections and center my life around you in order to fall more deeply in love with you.

Ryan Adelman, *Psychology*
Cleveland, OH

"Holy Spirit, unite me to my

sisters and brothers

as you unite the Father and Son

in the oneness of your love."

Bernie Rochon

Psychology Professor

Lansing Community College

Whisper Fifty: Taking Off the Mask

> "Underneath my outside face, there's a face that none can
> see. A little less smiley, a little less sure,
> but a whole lot more like me."

This Shel Silverstein quote essentially described who I was. I could put on a different mask at a moment's notice depending on whom I was spending time with or whom I was trying to impress, morphing myself into whatever others wanted me to become. One day, I realized how utterly unhappy I was, because I had always made the choice to hide. I decided to make a change during junior year of high school by attending Kairos, a four-day retreat my school holds each year.

Through hearing various speeches and taking part in activities, I gradually began to let my guard down, letting others see the real me. For as long as I can remember, I always tried my best to appear perfect to those around me. I stifled who I was to please others in an attempt to get them to like me. Although I had countless personality masks, Kairos was the catalyst for change in my life. Numerous times before, I saw myself as a broken person, thinking I was the only one who struggled with insecurity and self-doubt. I never thought people that I viewed as perfect were dealing with the same issues that I was. At the end of my junior year, I was presented with a wonderful opportunity; I had been chosen to lead Kairos senior year. This led me to an even greater level of personal realization and a deeper relationship with God.

I began senior year with weekly meetings to plan the pinnacle of Lansing Catholic retreats. We divided up responsibilities, and I was given the task of preparing a talk called "Know Yourself." Since I had been to Kairos already, I thought I could write it quite easily. I sat down to write and began to lose sight of the goal. I constantly asked myself, "What will my classmates think if I share this?" I was so fearful of becoming vulnerable to people who were just like me, full of doubt, insecurity and worry. I finally got the courage to continue and wrote eighteen pages without stopping. There were moments when I wanted to edit something, but I made myself keep writing, as that was the only way I could write my story in the way it had to be told. I wrote through anger, heartbreaking sadness, utter shame, and fear, not stopping to wipe tears from my eyes even as I wrote the most difficult parts.

Giving my talk to my peers was much harder than I ever imagined it would have been. Shaking and scared, I stood in front of them and began to speak. After a few minutes, most of the fear subsided and I felt a sense of warmth come over me. While I spoke I felt as though the Holy Spirit spoke to me. All I could hear was, "Your imperfections and failings are what make you beautiful." As I transitioned into harder parts of my talk, I was at peace.

Throughout my youth, I thought I had to be what the world viewed as perfect. I was always hyper aware of how I looked. For years I wouldn't leave the house without putting makeup on. I made a big deal about how I dressed and the way clothing fit me. Looking back on it, I must have had body-image issues. Because of this image of perfection I worked so hard to portray, I often felt a false sense of superiority. I displayed a calm front, while inside I was screaming for help. All of this unnecessary stress took control over my life. I continued to pretend it was not a problem because I did not want to fall short of the harsh standard of perfection to which I held myself.

Through all my hopes, fears, joys, and struggles, I have become the person I am today. My life is my story and sharing it aids in making corrections and finding my faults. My Kairos experience let me unpack my heart, leaving behind the parts of myself that were a hindrance to the person that I am called to become. Learning to trust in God always and let my guard down has led me to happiness.

The Spirit Whispered: You are beautiful because of your differences and flaws. Until you love yourself, you will not be able to love others. Share what is on your heart with others, for nobody is meant to suffer alone. Walk through life with me, stride by stride, and I will bring you happiness.

Prayer: Divine Spirit, give me the strength to be my true self. Help me to see myself as you see me, perfect only in my imperfection. Present me with challenges that make it necessary for me to depend on you.

Anne Marie Dunneback, *Nursing*
Lansing, MI

"In the garden I tend to
drop my thoughts here and there.
To the flowers I whisper the secrets I keep
and the hopes I breathe.
I know they are there
to eavesdrop for the angels."

Dodinsky

Whisper Fifty-One: Jesus Take the Wheel

My Spirit whisper may be a little different than others. You see, I was eleven months old at the time this accident happened and I have only heard of this story from my mom and family.

My seventeen-year-old sister and I were riding in the car. She was driving and I was in a car seat in the back. We had just picked up our van from a campground where my dad and brothers were biking home. My mom was following us in our van. She was behind us close enough to see our car until we went over a hill and just barely out of her sight. As my mom was coming over the hill, she could not see our car. The car had disappeared. My mom's stomach dropped. She saw a truck smoking in the middle of the road, but no car was to be found. It took her a moment to realize there had been a collision between the car I was in and the truck. She was in a panic when she was unable to find our car.

She continued to look around until she saw our mangled vehicle laying upside down in an adjacent house's yard. Never in her life had my mom been happier to hear an infant crying. She ran up to the scene and found us there alive.

There is no doubt in my mind our guardian angels were hard at work that day. With no other part of the car salvageable, and having rolled over nearly two times, it was nothing short of a miracle that my sister and I walked away with hardly a scratch.

This accident gives me a personal reminder to never take a moment of life for granted. I feel that my life was saved for a reason and God is not finished with my time on earth. As a student at Michigan State I became involved with St. John Student Center by leading Women's Group and retreats.

I feel this is my way of letting God's will be done and not my own, as he continues to work incredibly in my life and in those around me in this amazing community.

The Spirit Whispered: I am not finished with you yet.

Prayer: Divine Spirit, let me not take a moment of this precious life for granted, which you so graciously granted to me through love, that I may do your will and all things in your glory.

Alyssa Klein, *Kinesiology/Pre-Chiropractic Major*
Pewamo, MI

"'It's impossible.' said Pride.

'It's risky.' said Experience.

'It's pointless.' said Reason.

'Give it a try.'

Whispered the Heart."

Author Unknown

Whisper Fifty-Two: God Speaks?

During winter break my mom and I decided to go to the movies because the weather was just too cold to do anything else. She had wanted to see Maleficent because her favorite actress, Meryl Streep, was starring in it. I, like most college students, heard her say "free movie" and had my boots on within minutes. Behind all of the singing and dancing, the plotline of Maleficent was rather unusual. I began to learn about the back-story from all of my favorite childhood fairy tales. The writers integrated the stories of Jack and the Bean Stalk, Little Red Riding Hood and Cinderella so well that I thought I was seeing something completely new. On the ride home I started to think about my childhood and how this new movie made all of my old memories seem a bit more fulfilled. Strangely, I felt as if a piece from my childhood was being put back into the puzzle of my memories that I never knew was missing. Even more so, the movie reminded me of my freshman year in college and how one man changed my thoughts about Jesus.

To give you a picture of who I was my freshman year, most people would describe me as a pretty intense student, who knew that school and God were the two most important parts of her life. I was (and still am) a social butterfly who truly enjoyed making others feel uplifted because that was how God made me feel. So, as I was walking through campus, I came across a tall dark man who was preaching at the corner of a building. The building is Wells Hall and the man is formally known as the "Wells Hall Preacher." A group of people go there to preach the Gospel. However, their tactics are to shame students into feeling hopeless. They call students out on their sins and speak of a wrathful God who casts judgment on all (all of course, except for them). As I walked past them, I stopped with my friend to listen because I heard the name Jesus Christ. It was the first of many encounters with this man and I was absolutely in shock. He was saying things about Jesus I didn't believe and quoting scripture, reciting verses I never even knew were in the Bible. My heart began to stir. I felt a pushing from inside and how did I respond? "No, No, No..." I told God, "I don't want to say anything, and I'm scared. I know you, why do I need to say anything? What if people judge me? What if... what if...?" Then a stranger said to me, "Hey you should speak up, he sounds insane!" Was that God? I think so. So I did, I said to the Wells Hall preacher, "Yeah that Corinthian book is from the Old Testament!"

For anyone who doesn't know, the book of Corinthians is from the New Testament. Boy was I wrong and I felt awful. I had a red face, sweaty palms, I wanted to hide myself in a small closet forever type of feeling. Then he responded to me, "No. You are wrong and YOU need to read your Bible before you can say anything to me." That felt like a slap in the face.

He was right though. The crazy man who said nothing but terrible things to students was right about me. At first I thought, "No way do I need to read anything. I know that the Father, the Son and the Holy Spirit all love me. What do I need to read scripture for? I feel secure in my own heart and that is good enough." But then when I began to think about what I actually knew of Jesus, it started to sound like a fairy tale. My idea of him was this man, born in extraordinary circumstances with unthinkable challenges all dying for us and for our salvation. He was resurrected and now is with the Father. Outside of those sentences, I couldn't tell you what scripture had to say about him.

I think this fairy tale image of Christ plagues many Christians today. Figuratively speaking, if Christianity were a profession, and whether or not you were offered a job was based solely on your knowledge of Jesus, most of us would not be hired. As a student planning to go to medical school, I wonder how much effort I have put into my schooling before receiving my acceptance letter. I have spent countless hours studying, countless cups of coffee, and countless fill-in-the-bubble tests to be equipped for medicine. I know it is not good enough to shadow my family doctor to call myself a physician. If that were the case, I would be worried as I am sure you probably would be. So then, to you my reader, whoever you may be and at whatever stage you are at with God, do you think it is enough to shadow your pastor to call yourself a disciple? Is it enough to watch your peers to know about the things Jesus Christ did for you? Will your parents show you through their actions what exactly was said during the Last Supper and about death that Jesus endured? Why do we turn away from the Bible? Is it boring to us? Are God's divine words not enough for us? For me at least, I never turned away from the Bible because I never even looked at the Bible.

Spending time reading the Bible is spending time with God. Every morning, I try to read a little bit from scripture. I am telling you this truly from a humble heart because I can promise you that each time I open scripture, I never leave without something added to my own image of God. In four years at Michigan State University, I began to fill in the gaps of my fairy tale, image of God. My life was not boxed in a fairy tale so I stopped putting him in that box. I realized that God has always been with me and that do not need to be a scripture scholar to learn something about him. Why is this? Two reasons: 2 Timothy 3:16 and John 14:26.

"All scripture is inspired by God and is useful for teaching, for refutation, for correction and for training in righteousness, so that one who belongs to God may be competent, equipped for every good work." 2 Timothy 3:16

"The Advocate, the Holy Spirit that the Father will send in my name, he will teach you everything and remind you of all that I told you." John 14:26

Jesus is called a teacher for a reason and he is also called the living Word. The Bible is not stagnant nor is it an outdated book filled with material not relatable to our lives. Everything we experience daily has a direct link to the Bible. We just do not read it enough to see how applicable it is to our lives. We learn how to become disciples in the world when faced with these challenges. God is truly with us, he chose all of the broken people in the past to fulfill His promise. Who knows, perhaps you may discover where you fit within the Bible. The more I read from either the Old or New Testament, the words come alive and I begin to make connections between books. I understand scripture from the eyes of God because the Holy Spirit guides me while I read.

God has given us a versatile and applicable book. Only two actions are truly necessary for reading scripture. When I open my book I say,

157

"God, what do you want to show me today? Please help my heart be open to you."

The Bible is all about relationships between people. God will talk to you through scripture. So often we tell him what we need, want and think while rarely leaving time for him to speak. Spend a little time in scripture. God will reveal himself to you in ways that touch your heart. For my last question to you, if you were standing in front of that Wells Hall preacher, how would you respond?

The Spirit Whispered: Dive into my living word.

Prayer: Divine Spirit, fly into the depths of my heart so that I may be open to listening to your word.

Theresa Kaminski, *Genomics and Molecular Genetics*
Lake Orion, MI

Whisper Fifty-Three: What Happened to My Friend Sarah

I used to be a member of the marching band in high school. A dear friend of mine, Sarah, passed away in a tragic car accident just a mile away from my house – it was awful to lose such a close friend. My friend Emily was also close with Sarah; we all played in the band together. Sarah and I always sat next to each other as she was an oboist and I a flautist.

It was one year after the accident, and I was really missing Sarah. I was sitting in the band room thinking about Sarah, but looking for Emily. Emily didn't show up to our second hour class. I was hoping Emily would miraculously be in our last class of the day. I took my seat feeling disappointed, but still hopeful. Someone behind me gave my chair a little kick. I turned to scold the perpetrator, but I recognized Emily's green brand named shoes. I turned around and looked at her quizzically. Emily gave me a piece of paper which read: "I promised Sarah I'd bring you to the cemetery."

Right after class we drove in to the cemetery, I had mixed feelings. This was my first visit since the funeral. I didn't know what to expect. After parking our car, Emily and I walked toward the grave. As we approached the grave site, there was a man standing there with a bucket of tools. We watched him as he put up her headstone.
The man, who was the grave keeper, asked us: "Would you girls mind telling me where the hole in the bottom part of this stone is so I can lower the spike in the top part into the concrete? I wouldn't want to lose another finger!" He had no idea that Sarah was our friend. Even though he was a stranger to us, we wanted to help him.

As the grave keeper was adjusting the headstone, he asked us to help seal the two pieces together by smoothing the compound. We finished the job. Our fingers were so messy, we wiped them on the grass. He began washing the dust and extra compound off of the stone and noticed the date. "She wasn't very old when she died was she?" he said, "I wonder what happened..." That's when I told him about the accident. "Too young," he responded shaking his head. He started washing Sarah's headstone again, but with reverence this time. He used every drop of the water in his pail to clean the stone and even watered Sarah's flowers with his own water bottle. This touched Emily and me deeply. After a few moments of all three of us staring at the stone in silence, he decided to leave, but we remained. This was a hard year for me. I lost a number of classmates, but Sarah was very special. I had never lost anyone in my family, let alone a dear friend like her. I did not know how to deal with the grieving I was experiencing. I did not know how long this grieving would last or how I could continue to hold the deep sadness in my heart. Visiting the cemetery that day helped give me some closure. I knew I was not alone. God knew what I needed and He knew which heart to send his whisper to. After this experience, I felt a sense of peace.

The Spirit Whispered: I guided you to the cemetery today to heal your broken heart. Trust that I will always be there for you. I will never disappoint you.

Prayer: Divine Spirit, open my heart to realize that there are no coincidences. You have placed every person, moment, and experience in my life for a reason that will become clearer as time passes. Allow me to appreciate your sensitivity to my feelings.

Christina Igl, *Arts and Humanities and Spanish*
Mason, MI

Whisper Fifty-Four: Growing Up and Growing in My Faith

Growing up Catholic, like most kids my age when I was younger, I went to church because my parents told me to and not because I wanted to. Whenever my parents had the one rare Sunday when they said we weren't going to Mass, I was secretly very happy, and I'll admit I felt guilty for a few seconds and then forgot about it. This is how it was for me up until I went on my first Life Teen retreat in the spring of ninth grade. After that something changed in me.

Fast forward four years, I went to college. College is where I really took control of faith. I went to Mass because I wanted to and not because I had to. If I went to Mass it was because I made the conscious effort to, my parents weren't waking me up to go. I had to make the decision to go and I did. I felt at home right away at my college's Catholic student center. St. John's became my new home and I loved the fact that I found a church close to me that I felt comfortable in.

My sophomore year I was at Sparticipation, which is a big event for freshmen and all students with different student organizations that you can be a part of on campus. I was running a booth for a club that I was in and had to go run an errand. I was walking through the crowd and this lady stopped me and said, welcome! "You look Catholic," and handed me a flyer and told me to come to their student Mass the next Tuesday night. I was completely caught off guard because I wondered what she meant, "I look Catholic." I'm not wearing anything that says I am. Hmm, maybe she saw my rosary ring on my necklace? I had no idea what made her think that I "Looked Catholic," but it made me smile because it was a good thing, a great thing actually. She made my day and had no idea that she did, but it made me feel good inside that something about me made her feel that I was Catholic.

Before I had wanted to attend one of the student Masses, but it was always late and didn't really want to ride my bike all that way by myself, so I never went. After this encounter, I decided I would go, especially since it was the beginning of the year, so it would be easier to transition to the group. I went to the Mass the following week, met some great people, and really felt uplifted by the end of the night.

I started biking to Mass on Tuesday and Thursday nights with people from my neighborhood and when we rode through campus, people would often turn their heads and say, "What, are they a bike gang?" or "Whoa, look at all those people!" because there would be at least eight to twelve of us all biking to Mass from my neighborhood alone. It was kind of a joke to us that we were Jesus' biker gang, but we really looked like one and it was funny.

Going to Mass three times a week is something I never thought of, especially if you would have told me that when I was little. Yet here I was, a sophomore in college going to Mass three times a week. One of my roommates didn't understand it even though she was Catholic, and even my mom was rather surprised. I'll admit that I surprised myself, and even though some weeks, due to school conflicts, I may have attended only one student Mass. However, the days I had to miss, I felt different. Going to Mass gave me such a fulfillment and joy that I have a hard time describing it at first. On top of that I was making friends with the other students in the parish, and growing closer to God every single day. St. John's Student Center is truly my other home when I am here at school. I am from Texas and don't have any family here, the closest people to me were my teammates from my university's equestrian team, but soon enough everyone at St. John's became my family to.

Now I can't forget the lady who stopped me that day and told me that I looked Catholic; she turned out to be the sister from the parish. She has definitely helped me to feel at home. She has this aura that makes you want to be around her and be more like her in your faith life. Sister Dorothy has been my light in the church, she encourages me to push myself spiritually and grow closer to Jesus. We can all take charge of our faith and make it what we want, and achieve the relationship with Jesus Christ that we desire. The retreats that I go on, along with the community that I am a part of due to my parish, have helped me to grow in my faith as I continue to grow up and grow as a person.

The Spirit Whispered: Listen to me my child and I will guide you and show you the way. I will surround you with people who will help you in your journey.

Prayer: Divine Spirit, please guide me to follow the will of God. Give me peace of mind. Help me to listen to your will. I am your servant and am here to serve you.

Shannel Cacho, *Animal Science*
Plano, TX

"Intellectual rationalizing all
disappears when the
Holy Spirit
touches your life."

Joseph Guzman
Human Resources and Labor Relations
Social Science at MSU

Whisper Fifty-Five: Jesus, Is That Really You?

From the time of my First Communion as a child, I knew there was something special about what we ate and drank at church. I can still recall the feeling of excitement I had at my first Holy Communion. I remember feeling God's presence in a new way as I returned back to my pew after receiving Jesus. I also remember actually looking forward to going to church because I could receive Communion! But after a few weeks went by, receiving Communion didn't seem like such a special thing anymore. I had grown accustomed to the practice and the times when I would forget to fold my hands in line or say "Amen" before receiving communion, a nudge or word from my dad served as a reminder of what we were doing. Receiving Holy Communion at Mass on Sundays was really the only time I encountered Jesus present in his precious Body and Blood. Needless to say, when you only spend time with someone for a few minutes each week, it's difficult to get to know them, and this was true for Jesus and me.

I continued going to Sunday Mass my first year at Michigan State University; however, I was hesitant to get any more involved. The self-image I was trying to cultivate in college made me cautious about being associated with "church people." After grudgingly accepting an invitation to go on a weekend retreat through the student parish, I found myself awestruck while hearing a personal testimony of God's love in action. Immediately after the talk, I escaped into the chapel and, through the grace of God, I burst into tears and laughter as my heart overflowed with joy at the realization that Jesus is for real.

Just a couple of months after the retreat, I went to South Carolina and worked as a summer intern for a steel company. Upon arriving, I was excited to learn that I would be living with another Catholic man my age. He had the same name as my brother, Nolan. Nolan quickly became a good friend who helped me to grow in my faith. Nolan let me borrow CDs with testimonies of faith related topics. One day on a drive home from work, I was listening to a CD entitled "Life-Changing Stories of the Eucharist" by Jesse Romero. As I passed St. Anthony's church, I decided to stop by because I remembered Nolan mentioning there was adoration of the Eucharist there every day. This was the first time I had ever heard of such a thing, and as I walked into the small chapel, I saw the host held in a shiny gold thing (which I later learned was called a monstrance). I got on my knees and asked, "Jesus, is that really you?" I wasn't sold on the idea that God was present in a little white wafer of bread, so I prayed for God to show me if that really was him.

I only visited that chapel a couple more times that summer and soon enough I was back home in Michigan. However, a few months later I found myself away from home, this time it would be for about eight months as I was taking a semester off school to co-op at a packaging company in Wisconsin. After my first Sunday Mass at Most Blessed Sacrament Parish in Oshkosh, I looked through the bulletin and was excited to see they had an adoration chapel open 24/7. I decided to start making a habit of visiting the chapel for one hour each week. This eventually became the best hour of my week, and I looked forward to going there each Thursday evening. The Director of Student Outreach at my parish once said that God dwells there in a very special way - different from his divine presence in nature or in other people. As the weeks and months went by, I became convinced without doubt that Jesus was not only spiritually, but also *physically* present in that chapel, as true God and true man. It is truly a special grace to discover Jesus' presence in the Eucharist!

The Spirit Whispered: Just be with me, don't worry about what to do or say, just be with me and listen to your heart.

Prayer: Divine Spirit, I believe that you are the one true God and that you sent your only begotten Son into this world for my sake. Help my unbelief. I pray that my devotion to you may increase, especially my devotion to you in the Most Holy Sacrament.

Riley O'Shea, *Materials Science and Engineering*
Grand Ledge, MI

Whisper Fifty-Six: Soul on Fire

I was confirmed in eighth grade, and for a Confirmation gift my grandpa (who was also my sponsor) gave me a book called "The Life of a Priest." He told me I should consider the priesthood. In my head, I was laughing hysterically thinking, "Yeah, right, not in a million years!"

I didn't think about the priesthood again until my senior year. At the time I was applying to West Point and I knew I was going to get accepted. I was at praise and worship and I knelt before the Lord in adoration and asked him to come to me. I saw him and myself in a cabin and he told me he wanted me to be a priest. I first thought that it was just me imagining things and there was no way that was actually God. Then I thought to myself, "Okay, if I don't get into West Point I might, possibly start thinking about becoming a priest." A month later I was denied admission into West Point.

Thus began my discernment at Michigan State. I tried to keep an open mind to whatever vocation God was calling me to. My freshmen year I started going to daily Mass. I joined priestly discernment group at St. John's, and I even started reading the bible! I also met a girl. She was pretty much perfect. She was conservative, liked country music, and was Christian. We would study together, but we wouldn't really study, we would just talk about God until two o'clock in the morning. While I was on fall retreat I couldn't get her out of my head. When I got back, I asked her out. It turned out that her friend from home had already asked her out and she needed to respect him asking her out first. A few weeks went by and the guy hurt her in some way and she decided she was going to fall back in love with God again before she started another relationship. At the same time I was offered to go on a priestly discernment pilgrimage on the Camino de Santiago in Spain. One of the requirements of going on this pilgrimage was that you couldn't be in a dating relationship.

I had to choose between two good things. Either I wait for this amazing girl or I start solely discerning the priesthood. I chose the latter. At first it was a struggle. My prayer was basically, "Lord, show me your will right now," and that wasn't working. I went into a period of desolation for a time where I didn't feel anything while I was praying. This lasted from the end of November until the end of January, when my friend and I went to the Shrine of the Little Flower. There I learned about St. Teresa of Lisieux. St. Teresa was fifteen years old when she became a nun and had a total child-like heart that was on fire for the Lord. Her story inspired me to do the same. I decided to just focus on loving the Lord with all of my being.

By focusing on loving God, he has shown me so much. He has given me a passion to serve His people. Now all I want to do is spread this fire that I have to everyone I meet and that is what attracts me to the priesthood. I was at daily Mass one day and the first reading was about the creation of Eve. When the priest, Father Dan, got up for his homily, I thought to myself, "There's no way this is going to apply to me because he's going to talk about marriage and I'm solely discerning the priesthood." But as his homily went on, my peripheral vision became blurrier and blurrier while Father Dan came more into focus. Then he said, "Saint Catherine of Siena said, 'Be who God meant you to be and you will set the world on fire.'" I was so full of the Spirit that I began weeping in the pew.

I am still discerning, but I feel called to the priesthood more each day. What I have found in this process is that the best way to discern God's will for us, is to fall head-over-heals in love with him and completely surrender ourselves to him. The Lord will work through this love that we have for him and make us souls on fire.

The Spirit Whispered: Set your heart on fire for God and hold nothing back. I will show you the way so be at peace and know you are doing God's will. Trust in me.

Prayer: Divine Spirit, light a fire in my heart for God. Give me the courage to totally surrender myself to the God of love. I want to do his will. Instill in me a thirst for him because I know he thirsts for me.

Matthew Kurt, *Political Theory and Constitutional Democracy Major*
Canton, MI

Whisper Fifty-Seven: The Holy Spirit through Spartan Spirit

I came to Michigan State University (MSU) in 1973 as a freshman from Flint, Michigan. Growing up in a family where three generations worked for General Motors, I was the first to attend college outside of General Motors Institute (GMI) now Kettering University. I knew in high school that I wanted to be in a service-oriented, people-oriented profession. My major was psychology and I wanted to help people through this profession. I had a great-uncle who was a missionary priest and his sister, my great-aunt, was a Sister of Mercy. I also had a great- aunt who was a Sister of St. Joseph and a cousin who is a cloistered Carmelite nun. The religious in my family gave me a great respect for those who chose this calling. I was very close to them and them to me and my family.

I thought about religious life in high school, most probably because of the influence of my aunts, uncle and cousin. But, I would quickly put the thought out of my mind thinking that God would call someone who was holier and more perfect than I. It did not dawn on me that maybe God worked in extra-ordinary ways through ordinary people until I was a Spartan at MSU. Most of the guys in my residence hall were Catholic, from Catholic schools and we attended Mass *most* weekends. Mass at St. John Church and Student Center had more energy than any church I had ever been to in my life. The priests and staff were "cool" as we said in the 70s and they spoke to our young minds and hearts.

The thought of the priesthood as a calling for *me* would not leave my mind, as much as I tried to push it away. There were two professors who I would see at Mass who influenced my faith. I had a psychology professor who had us read a Jesuit psychologist from the University of Chicago whose writings bridged psychology and spirituality. Another influence was a Humanities professor who taught a discipline, that I thought had nothing to do with my intentions in life, with great passion. I took all my electives in religious studies and philosophy. However, the thought of priesthood, while intriguing, did not make me happy. I had a great career in mind and looked forward to having a family and living out my faith like everyone else I knew.

169

One day after thinking again, "Mark, you ought to be a priest" I actually got mad and frustrated and skipped the class I was going to on campus and walked over to St. John's to pray about it. I remember telling the Lord, "I do not want to be a priest, but if You want me to be a priest I will. However, I am not taking any initiative!" I walked back to my apartment. Never dare God! The next week the diocesan vocation director started helping on the weekends at the student parish and we became fast friends. After a retreat for college men interested in priesthood and his advice to stay at Michigan State University and enter theology after graduation my thought was, "They won't like me or I won't like them." I knew I had to trust the inner voice that would not go away and at least try it out. After four great years of formation my happiness only grew whenever I thought and now felt, "Mark, you should be a priest."

I have spent 28 years of my life in Spartan Country. Four of the years were spent as a student until graduation in 1977. I returned in 1987 and served four years as the parochial vicar of the student parish where I found my vocation and first heard the whispers from the Spirit. I stayed in East Lansing for the following six years as diocesan vocation director. My first assignment as pastor was in Jackson, MI and lasted four years until I return to St. John's and Michigan State University as pastor in 2000. I often think of the holy irony of being here all these years. This is the place where God called me to priesthood and helped me to listen to that inner voice through priests, pastoral staff, professors, classmates and friends saying, "Trust me!"

The Spirit Whispered: You need to trust in me. I know the desire of your heart.

Prayer: Divine Spirit, open my mind and heart to the ways that you whisper your love and will through those around me! Amen.

Rev. Mark Inglot, *Pastor*
St. Thomas Aquinas Parish/St. John Church and Student Center
East Lansing, MI

Whisper Fifty-Eight: When the Going Gets Tough

I had the honor of giving the closing talk at our Undergrad Spring retreat themed "Encounter." The retreat was aimed at helping the retreatants become more familiar and engaged with the various ways that the Catholic Church helps us encounter the Risen Lord, whether that be through adoration, Mass, reconciliation, community, praise and worship, or small group. As the last talk, it was my job to wrap everything up and to come up with some lasting advice that would not only reinforce what was said on the retreat but to emphasize ways to keep the retreat "high" going; to give them practical advice on how to maintain their faith post-retreat. I would like to share with you how I concluded the Encounter Retreat. A lot of times in religious friend groups we see this trend of people who remain happy in the midst of suffering. This suffering can take shape in varying degrees—it can be the death of a loved one, a terminal illness, work-related stress, anxiety about the future, the lack of time to get everything done—yet we still see this common theme of happy, suffering Christians. Sounds like an oxymoron to me, suffering and happy? Yup! That then begs the question, "Why?" Why do we see these people who suffer remain happy in spite of all their pain? What do they have that gets them to that point?

What I really think this boils down to is that these people had a personal relationship with God and that personal relationship with God was the foundation of everything for them. As cliché of an analogy as it might be, a great example of this is the parable in the Gospels where Jesus tells the story of a house built on solid ground and a house built on sandy ground. When the rains came, the winds blew and the flood waters gushed through, it was the house planted on solid ground that stood the trial. Likewise with those happy, suffering Christians, their foundation is the one built on solid ground and that solid ground is rooted in a personal relationship with Jesus Christ. However, I would be remiss if I did not mention that on top of this relationship with Jesus, these people also had trust in that relationship, because without trust there really is no solid relationship. This trust is such a key component of this relationship because more times than not in our faith life we do not understand what is happening to us, we feel lost, and we have no clue where

God wants us to go. However, by trusting in that personal relationship with him, our foundation will stand firm come the trials of life.

So how do you maintain that relationship with God when the going gets tough? Just like human relationships, our relationship with God is not something that achieves "best friend status" overnight, or even over days. This relationship takes time to grow. However, even though this can't happen overnight, there are steps we can take to make sure our foundation is setting correctly and that our house is being put up properly. So I would like to give you three solid ways to aid in that process:

1. You aren't in this alone.
2. Find practical ways to maintain your faith
3. Define the path/ know your mission

First point, you aren't in this alone.
I realize how basic this idea seems. You are probably saying in your head, "No, Katie. I realize I am not the only human on the planet." True, but sometimes I would argue that we do a great job of acting like that. A lot of times when troubles come and we should be relying on the help of others, we come up with excuses such as "I don't want to be a burden," or "They won't understand." God did not create us to be solitary creatures and we should not act as such.

In the Gospels, you see Jesus sending out his disciples two by two. Notice this sense of community and companionship for the journey. When you read the story of Jesus picking his apostles, he doesn't just stop at Peter because he is the rock on which the Church is going to be built. No, Jesus picks Peter and eleven others to help him out. Looking at church teaching today, there is this awesome concept of the Communion of Saints, that at every Mass not only is the physical church united, but the entire earthly church is united. We humans have an *amazing* community surrounding us! One of the great ways that I have found helpful in tapping into this gift of community is through having accountability partners. The gist of this exercise is that you find at least one person to hold you accountable for whatever it is you need accountability for. This could include things such as vices you struggle with, academic goals for the semester, and general life goals. Just as a quick personal example: A couple weeks ago I was sitting on my couch talking to my roommate, one of my accountability partners, about the 501 reasons why I should get into a graduate school I was applying to. My roommate, knowing that one of my weaknesses is pride, called me out on it and said, "Hey, this is what I am hearing: maybe you should pray for some humility today." While some people may think that she was out of line or was too forward, I appreciated her keeping me accountable.

As great as all these human resources are for us, humans are human and well, even with the greatest of intentions we can still screw up pretty big. And God realizes that, so not only does he give us each other, but he also gives us himself as a companion for this journey. He is there for us through thick and thin and he never leaves our side. I would like to emphasize that, **you are not in this alone!** Utilize the gift of community and relationships that God has given you on this faith journey.

Second Point: Find practical ways to sustain your faith.
How many times do we catch ourselves putting God on the back burner because we are too busy or too tired? If we are pointing fingers, I am guilty as charged. The sad thing about this, though, is that I would not do that to my earthly friends. I would be a better steward of my time so that I would be able to be fully present to my friends when I was going to spend time with them. So too, should we treat our relationship with God. We need to find those ways that bring us closer to God and to stick with them. For instance, I really connect to God through Mass and Eucharistic Adoration. Because I know that, I make it a priority to engage in those activities at least once a week because I know that those things are the fuel for my relationship with God. I want to encourage you to do the same. Find a couple ways that you really mesh with God and pursue those. Make them a priority in your life and let them continue to help you grow in your relationship with God.

Third and Final Point: Define the path, find your mission.
A lot of times we hear about our "faith journey" or "path of life." I really enjoy these analogies and I would like to point out three key aspects of a path or being on a journey. First, there is always a starting point and an end point. Second, there are always boundaries defining the path. These boundaries may be well defined or not defined at all but there are still markers out there that let you know when you are on the path, straying off the path, or completely off the path. Thirdly, there is always an intentionality of the person on the path. Even if the path is unknown, the end unclear, or whatever unknown variable there is, there is still the intention to take the next step, or even to stay put.

I would like to encourage you to assess where you are right now in your faith life, and come up with a plan for where you want to be in the future. Define that end goal. Put up boundaries for your path. Create an intentionality to follow that path. This past summer I read a book that inspired me to do just that for my own faith life. In John R. Wood's book, "Ordinary Lives, Extraordinary Mission," he talks about how we are all in this huge spiritual battle for our souls and points out that if we are on an ultimate journey to heaven there are two things we need to do. One, we need to acknowledge that we are in this battle, and two, we need to come up with a plan to get through this battle. John encourages his readers to create mission statements that outline where you want to be in your faith life so that you can define a path that will help you achieve your mission. Having done this myself, I highly recommend it! So many times I have gone back to my mission statement months after I first wrote it thinking I was going to change something and found that it all still applied to my future goals in life. Take some time to prayerfully consider where you want your relationship with God to be and where you want it to go. Write down your plan and stick to it.

I am a Kinesiology Major at Michigan State. Going into the summer between my junior and senior year of college I was very much set on applying to Physical Therapy School, going to Physical Therapy school, and eventually becoming a Physical Therapist. However, that began to change when, at the end of the summer, I began to seriously discern a potential vocation and career in Church ministry.

I'll spare you all the drama and overanalyzing that plagued the greater part of my first semester of senior year, but I do want to emphasize a few things:

- I took advantage of the community God gave me. I involved a lot of people in this discernment process—my parents, my friends, my accountability partners, my campus minister and academic advisors.
- I utilized one of the ways that I connect with God. I made it a priority to go to Adoration.
- I defined my mission—not only did I have my own personal mission statement. I came up with a list of things that I wanted that would impact my future career choice. I labeled the list, "Everything I want, I lay it down." I was letting Jesus make the call.

Because of the utilization of those three points, I can confidently say I have arrived at a decision that is taking me on the path that God is calling me to. I am attending Grand Valley State University to pursue a doctorate in Physical Therapy.

I challenge you to continually encounter Jesus in a real and personal way, and never give up in seeking to grow in your relationship with God.

As my classmate, Clinton Korneffel said, "The only constant in your life is Jesus—he encounters you daily, but it's up to you whether or not you acknowledge that encounter that makes a difference in your life."

The Spirit Whispered: Remember what St. Catherine of Sienna said, "You, O Eternal Trinity, are a deep ocean into which the more I penetrate, the more I discover and the more I discover, the more I seek you." I know you will continue to seek me.

Prayer: Divine Spirit, give me the strength to continually encounter you—whether through trials or joys in life. Provide me with the courage and strength to continue along on my journey with you so that I may grow closer to you.

Katie Collins, *Kinesiology*
Grand Rapids, MI

Here are some of the Mission Statements the Students wrote on our Spring Retreat "Encounter" 2015. You may be inspired to write your own.

My Mission

"Rise, then, for this is your duty! We will stand by you, so have courage and take action!" Ezra 10:4

I want to love Jesus. I want to see him in the people, places, and events I encounter in my daily life. I want to appreciate everything he does for me, in each of his little surprises and amazing gifts, and maintain a constant conversation with him, seeking advice and sharing the joys and sorrows of the day. I want to always keep my heart open to his infinite love, and leave behind anything that keeps me from him. I want to see him as my lover, as a spouse that actively pursues me and is eagerly waiting for me to spend time with him. I want to remain always faithful to him, and hold nothing back.

I want to regularly seek God in the Sacraments. In the Mass, I want to be completely present and vulnerable as I listen to His word and witness His sacrifice. And when I approach the altar, I want to see the groom waiting excitedly, and whole-heartedly accept his invitation to give my life to him as he has done for me. And when I stray from his way, when I am unfaithful and hurt myself, the people around me, and my Lord and Savior, I want to trust in His endless mercy and his powerful desire for me to return home. I want to rush back to his embrace, and understand that he will meet me exactly where I am in my faith journey, no matter what.

I want to build community—a group of friends and companions with whom I can share my questions, struggles, and triumphs. People who can hold me accountable for my academic, professional, and, most importantly, spiritual goals and actions that contribute to the accomplishment of these goals in my faith journey.

I want to know my faith. I want to always be studying and learning about God, through the Bible, his saints, the church's teachings, and other inspired authors and speakers that have experiences and advice to share.

I want to give over my mind and heart so they may no longer be slaves to pride, envy, lust, sloth, and self-loathing. I want to practice courage, wisdom, chastity, temperance, faith, patience, hope, and optimism, even if just one virtue at a time. I want to maintain a mental state free from sin of all kinds, and keep my emotions rooted in love of God, neighbor, and self.

I don't want to make excuses anymore: that I have too little time, talent, or treasure, so as to insult the one who granted me these gifts. Rather, I want to utilize them in any way I can to help others. Let there be no opportunities to give of myself that passed me by.

Even if I no longer feel a closeness or intimacy with Jesus, even if I feel separated from him in any way, I want to continue to encounter and learn about the Father, Son, and Holy Spirit. I want to never give up trying to improve my faith and improve my relationship with him, because that is what true love is.

Jackie Thelen

My Mission

I want to love Jesus with my entire being. I want to turn away from my idols and leave behind my notion of looking for other things, but instead to first and foremost seek God.

I want to love God and in turn receive his love and to honestly believe that my worth is based off of him alone, not anything the world can provide. I want to go where my trust has no borders, where I can joyfully follow the future God has planned for me with no fear or doubt.

I want to be the best version of myself. I want to approach God and the world with the heart and eyes of a child. I want to accept my gifts and give them back to God. I want to feel God being with me always. I am a cherished daughter of God. I want to run into the embrace of Jesus and hear the words, "Well done, my child. Welcome home."

Kristin Collins

My Mission

I want to always be worthy of God's grace and love. I want to show that love to others through my words and actions. I don't want to ever miss an encounter with God, whether he is speaking to me or using me to speak to another.

I want to be open to God's plan for me. I want to not worry so much and trust that God is leading me to great things. I want to have the courage to always say "yes" to all that God asks of me.

One day I want to have kids, and I want to be able to tell them about God using personal stories. I want to raise them to know God as I know him, as a friend.

Allison Linder

My Mission

I strive to never settle and be comfortable in my relationship with God. I want to find him in unexpected places and seek him in different ways every day.

I never want to deceive myself by buying into the lie that my faith has reached its capacity. Nor do I want to give into the mentality that 'I will never be perfect in my faith life, so why even try?'

I desire to be courageous enough to accept failure, and wise enough to gain understanding from my struggles.

I know God accepts me fully for who I am (good and bad) and loves me even when I struggle to love myself.

I want to find joy in every situation and be open to recognize God's goodness in every moment.

I want to share the gifts and talents that God has blessed me with to love and care for others in a way that is reflective of God's love for them.

I aspire to show God's goodness to others through example by standing up for those who can't stand up for themselves. I want to reach out and encourage those who are seen as inferior and highlight their strengths.

I want to trust that God's plans for me are far greater than anything I could dream of, and that he will guide me down the right path if I let him.

In all that I accomplish, I want to put aside my own ego and be able to give all the glory and praise to God.

Katie Theriault

My Mission

I never want to go through the motions. I want passion, reason and the Holy Spirit to direct my actions in the Church—whether personal or ministerial. I want to avoid the plague of being lukewarm.

I want to make a difference, whether in ministry, physical therapy, as a mother, or whatever I may be called to. I want to use my God given gifts for God's glory and to positively impact others, my community and the world. I want to change the world.

I want to learn to willingly accept crosses, to maybe even love them. I want to be able to joyfully suffer patiently. I want to master the virtues of courage, wisdom, patience, love and humility while conquering the vices of fear, gluttony, impatience, anger, and pride.

I want to be a saint. I want to overcome human weakness with God's help and become the saint and woman God created me to be.

I want to be strong in my faith, to remain forever curious, I want to remain childlike. I want to be in the world but not of it.

I want to be free. I don't want to be slave to food or drink or material pleasures. I want to learn to trust and love unconditionally.

I want to give this fight of faith the best I can give; I want to leave this world with nothing left to give, but open to receive all the graces of Heaven.

I want to walk this life giving all the glory to God, being forever grateful for the gifts I have been given and using those gifts to the best of my abilities. I want to come home to the words "Well done, good and faithful servant."

Kathryn Elizabeth Thomas More Collins

"What was personified in the body of Jesus
was a manifestation of this one universal truth:
Matter is, and has always been,
the hiding place for Spirit,
forever offering itself to be discovered anew."

Richard Rohr

Index of Citations